375

Schools Council
Research Studies

n

Schools Council
Research Studies

Curriculum Evaluation Today: Trends and Implications

Edited by David Tawney

A second collection of papers from members of
the Schools Council project evaluators'
group on aspects of their work

Macmillan Education

First published 1976

SBN 333 19743 7 Boards
SBN 333 18559 5 Limp

Published by
MACMILLAN EDUCATION LTD
London and Basingstoke

Associated companies and representatives throughout the world

Printed in Great Britain by
Hazell Watson & Viney Ltd
Aylesbury, Bucks

Foreword

It is the Schools Council's policy to make provision for the evaluation of all its curriculum development projects. In the case of large projects, this usually means appointing an evaluator, or even an evaluation team. In the case of small projects, it is normal for one member of the team to accept responsibility for the evaluation element. During the past seven years, these evaluators have met together at least three times a year to discuss a wide range of evaluation issues, to exchange ideas and information and to establish close personal contacts. They have also held two residential conferences.

It was this evaluators' group which produced *Evaluation in Curriculum Development: Twelve Case Studies*. This was written in 1969 and 1970, and the evaluators concerned were then 'thinking aloud' as they evolved their roles. It was thus very dated before it was published, and the evaluators' group has been anxious to produce another publication which would reflect the changes that have taken place in recent years in evaluation theory and practice. A large number of visitors to the Council, from both home and overseas, have shown a deep interest in evaluation, and many have expressed the hope that the sort of information they have been given orally will appear in print as soon as possible. This publication is therefore a response to a frequently expressed need. It was planned by a working party of the evaluators' group, which met regularly to resolve questions of content, arrangement and presentation. The authors are senior members of the group who, as a result of their practical work in the field, have accumulated a considerable expertise and wealth of experience. All except the author of Chapter 6, reviewing some completed evaluation studies, and the authors of the paper included as Chapter 5 have served the Council in an evaluation capacity.

Before the work started, a great deal of thought was devoted to the intended readership. Initially the intention was to direct the publication principally at newly appointed evaluators, teachers on secondment to diploma and higher degree courses, students in initial training (particularly those taking curriculum development as a part of their course), university and college of education staff, and all the many research workers who are involved in curriculum development both here and overseas. However, the needs and interests of practising teachers were always borne in mind with a view to a wider reader-ship. It is hoped that teachers, administrators and others who are interested in evaluation will find the work useful and stimulating. In particular, it could be used by those groups of teachers meeting in teachers' centres who are interested in evaluation problems.

The evaluation of curriculum development is of considerable interest and importance. This book considers various aspects of the important issues, many of which are complex and controversial. The Council is pleased to make it available as a source of information and a stimulus to further discussion.

Contents

Tables and figures

Tables

Figures

Acknowledgements

The Schools Council and the publisher wish to thank the Department of Education and Science and the Programme Committee of the National Development Programme in Computer Assisted Learning, for permission to include the quotation on p. 128, and F. E. Peacock Publishers, Inc., for permission to include the diagram on p. 15, from D. L. Stufflebeam et al., *Educational Evaluation and Decision Making* (1971).

1 Curriculum evaluation— definition and boundaries

Keith Cooper

'Evaluation' has come to have different meanings, which are reflected in the use of the specialized term 'curriculum evaluation'. Is the function of the curriculum evaluator to provide information for those making educational decisions, or should he also make judgements based on his findings? What is the nature of the information and the judgement? Is it, in fact, realistic to separate these aspects? How far is an evaluation restricted to a particular project or phase, and how far could it have wider application? What is the distinction between evaluation and research? A consideration of its specific character can provide us with a working definition.

'Evaluation' has become one of the current catchwords in educational parlance. Unfortunately for the clarity of our thought, however, the word is used in a number of different ways. This confusion in thought has led to a confusion in practice, particularly in the case of curriculum evaluation. It may be helpful to both thought and action, therefore, to try to unravel some of the ways in which this term is being used, and some of the implications for curriculum evaluation of adopting particular definitions.

There would seem to be at least two different senses in which evaluation is used, which might help to illuminate some of the difficulties of its use in the term 'curriculum evaluation'. The first is *evaluation as an ability or skill.* Bloom (1956), in his categorization of possible intellectual objectives, uses evaluation as the label for the class of objectives concerned with the pupil's ability to make 'judgments about the value . . . of ideas, works, solutions, methods, material, etc.' (p. 185). This sense has been followed by many other writers concerned with the same task. Guilford (1959) uses evaluation as the highest order of intellectual operations; T. C. Barrett (Clymer, 1972, p. 59) has proposed a 'Taxonomy of the Cognitive and Affective Dimensions of Reading Comprehension', which puts evaluation as a high-level category, below only appreciation. In Barrett's view, 'evaluation deals with judgement, and focuses on qualities of accuracy, acceptability, desirability, worth or probability of occurrences'. Similarly, the project on History, Geography and Social Science 8–13* uses 'the ability to evaluate information' as one of the keystones of its list of intellectual skills (Blyth et al., 1972, p. 5).

A second sense, which is equally common, is *evaluation as the assessment and testing of students*. Very many of the texts on statistical techniques for devising and analysing tests for students have the word 'evaluation' in the title (for instance, Adams, 1964; Ahmann and Glock, 1958; Bradfield and Moredock, 1957; Gronlund, 1965). Others tend to use the term interchangeably with assessment or testing in the text. One example of this can be seen in Thorndike and Hagen (1969); the authors say (p. 30) that they have written a 'book dealing with educational and psychological measurement procedures', and state that 'evaluation of pupil progress is a major aspect of the teacher's job'. One writer (Stones, 1970) tries to distinguish between evaluation and assessment, but keeps the whole emphasis squarely in the area of assessment of performance (p. 16):

In this section, I propose an approach to the evaluation of student learning which I consider could help to improve present procedures. I stress 'evaluation' to try to shift the emphasis from the weighing of student performance by staff to the joint appraisal of the performance of both (as teacher and learner) by both.

Certain elements appear to be common to both these usages; in particular, they both imply the notion of *judgement*, and the notion of *valuing*. Where evaluation is thought of as an ability or skill, it is the individual (usually the individual student or pupil) who is concerned with both the valuing—that is, weighing the evidence and placing particular value on each of the parts— and the judgement—deciding which parts of the evidence are more credible and making the final choice between competing alternatives. Having weighed the evidence, the individual is expected to be able to make a judgement and, if necessary, to defend it. In the second instance, where evaluation is seen as assessment, the teacher is concerned with the two elements in a rather different way. First, some sort of standard has to be constructed—that is, a value external to the student, as when the teacher is preparing a test for his own class, or even external to the school and independent of the teacher, as in a public examination like GCE O level or a standardized (e.g. intelligence) test. The task is then to relate the individual student to the external standard. When this valuing has been done, it is assumed that the information which emerges will help the teacher, or someone else such as an employer, to make judgements about the relative merits or abilities of individual students.

Curriculum evaluation can perhaps be seen more clearly when set in this context. Obviously, there are differences in the area of concern. As it has been

* Details of the British curriculum projects mentioned in the course of this book, including the names of the funding agencies, are given alphabetically by name of project on pp. 159–67.

used, curriculum evaluation refers in the main to judgements made about educational process (what happens in schools)—though judgements about product (what students have learned) may also be included. 'Curriculum' here has usually been taken to mean any educational practice which is assumed to affect the student's learning, from a new way of teaching algebra to the introduction of a new timetable. There has, however, been considerable disagreement over the way in which the valuing should be carried out, and also over who should actually make the judgement.

The growth of curriculum evaluation as a specialization within education has been the result of a desire to base judgements on more reliable evidence. Once again there have been two distinct points of view. One, which might be said to correspond to the idea of assessment, can be described as 'the measurement of the achievement of objectives'. The other, perhaps more akin to the idea of evaluation as a skill, can be summed up as 'the collection and provision of information about an educational situation'. (The origins, and some of the consequences, of these views are set out in Chapter 3; the aim here is to explore them with the idea of arriving at a more acceptable and workable definition of curriculum evaluation.)

The first of these positions was for a long time accepted as the ideal for curriculum evaluation. As Hastings (1966, p. 27) put it:

The most commonly held idea of the sequence of evaluation endeavors starts with the act of stating the objectives of a set of materials—a full course, a unit of some sort, or a group of several units. This is followed by the definition of these objectives, in behavioral terms. Next comes the development of items, that is, situations which call for the behavior defined. These items are combined into scorable units, scores are obtained on appropriate samples of youngsters. Then, finally, the sequence ends in attempts to interpret these scores in terms of the extent to which the new materials have developed the behaviors which satisfy the purposes the innovators had in mind.

One exponent of this attitude is Scriven (1967); he suggests (p. 40) that evaluation 'consists simply in gathering and combining of performance data with a weighted set of goal scales to yield either comparative or numerical ratings; and in the justification of (a) the data-gathering instruments, (b) the weightings, and (c) the selection of goals'.

A number of writers have found, however, that this notion of evaluation was much too restricting for practical activity. Hastings (1966), after stating the 'accepted' view, remarks (p. 27): 'A bit of experience in this area on a real job of evaluation will convince anyone that the steps of this total procedure— as simple as they are to state—are laden with problems of several kinds'. An early recognition that these problems stem partly from an inadequate conception of the scope of evaluation seems to have been Cronbach's paper, 'Course improvement through evaluation' (1963). His definition of evaluation marked a radically different approach: 'To draw attention to its full range of functions, we may define "evaluation" broadly as the *collection and use of information to make decisions about an educational program*' (p. 672). The implication is that there is more to evaluate in an educational programme than its stated objectives, however behavioural. This approach was also adopted by the recent Phi Delta Kappa National Study Committee on Evaluation (Stufflebeam et al., 1971, p. 40): 'Evaluation is the process of delineating, obtaining and providing useful information for judging decision alternatives'.

It will have been apparent that the Stufflebeam definition raises another problem. The list of activities included under the heading of evaluation makes no mention of actually taking the decision, or making the judgement, for which the evidence is produced. There is a difference here between the two sides. Those relying on an assessment approach—an appeal to an external standard, such as pre-specified objectives—have tended to suggest that, once the comparison with the standard has been made, the judgement follows more or less automatically; and that it is the person who has made the comparison who should go on to make his judgement explicit. On the other hand, those who are concerned with providing information for decision-making see a clear distinction between the collection of the evidence and the act of judgement which comes from it. This is in part because of the complex nature of educational decision-making, but mainly because of the position which education holds in the public domain. (This is discussed more fully in Chapter 2.) Decisions about education are rarely based only on 'objective' evidence; they must also take into account such notions as competing values or political practicability. It is suggested that education is part of a larger political system, for which the community has designated in various ways those people who have the responsibility—and the accountability—for making decisions about the allocation of public resources. It is not up to others to usurp this function.

This distinction, between provision of information and the making of judgements, may sound very unrealistic to the classroom teacher, who has the task of collecting his own information before he makes his own decision. The idea of having an evaluator to provide the teacher with information may move him to envy, or merely to laughter. Nevertheless, it may help the teacher to consider his task as though it were two separate activities. When he is collecting information, the teacher should be aware of the need to be as objective as possible; when he is making decisions, he should be aware that he is acting as a professional who has been given certain responsibilities by the public. In the later discussion in this chapter, the emphasis will be on the evaluator as having a distinct role; it must be kept in mind that what is said also applies to the teacher in his capacity as evaluator rather than decision-maker.

There has so far been little mention of British writing about evaluation. Until recently, there was very little to comment on. Published accounts of

actual evaluations, for instance, have had to wait until the curriculum development projects of the middle and late 1960s had come to an end. There have
been a few comments from those writing without this experience, and these
have basically accepted the 'achievement of objectives' approach, like Kerr
(1968, p. 25):

If the objectives of a course have been identified and described in concise
operational terms, it is logically a simple exercise to identify those aspects of a
course which it is desirable to evaluate and then to choose an appropriate
instrument or technique for each job.

The list of possible evaluation techniques which follows, however, is considerably wider than most 'traditional' evaluators would allow. Wiseman and
Pidgeon (1970) too are inconsistent, but in a different way. They adopt
Cronbach's definition of evaluation as the 'collection and use of information
to make decisions about an educational program'; but they then assume that
the only information collected will be about the achievement of objectives.

British practice, however, is very different in approach. Evaluators of major
projects have varied greatly in their approach but their focus has been almost
exclusively on provision of that information which decision-makers—either
the project team or potential users—might need. The interpretation of the
questions which the evaluator needs to answer has differed; see, for instance,
MacDonald (1973), whose focus is on users, and Harlen (1975), whose main
point of reference is the need for the project team to revise their progamme.
Perhaps the most comprehensive statement of the 'information provision'
viewpoint is in Crossland and Moore (1974, p. 6): 'Evaluation of the project itself
had to be based on those questions that persons external to it might ask.'
Harlen's work on Science 5–13 is particularly interesting in this context;
although the project adopted a framework of objectives, the evaluator felt
strongly that the range of information she provided must be much wider than
the extent to which the objectives were achieved. She was at least as much
interested in trying to gather evidence about *how* the project was used, and
why particular outcomes were observed.

Harlen's decision gives a pointer to the reasons why practitioners in evaluation have chosen to adopt a wider, more flexible working definition of curriculum evaluation. The measurement of the achievement of objectives can
yield very valuable evidence about a curriculum programme, but there is
much more to be said. If we wish to revise a programme under development,
it is no use knowing *what* an outcome is, if we have no idea *why*. If we wish
to make decisions about adopting a new programme, there are many questions about the implications of adoption which will rarely be noticed if the
evaluator takes a rigid, objectives-based stance. There are disadvantages to
using a wider approach, of course. For instance, when the evaluator has a
narrow focus, he can be much more confident about the accuracy of his data

because he is able to concentrate his time and resources. However, as Tukey (1963, p. 13) says of data analysis in general: 'Far better an appropriate answer to the right question, which is often vague, than an exact answer to the wrong question, which can always be made precise.'

One of the disadvantages of the wider definition of evaluation is that it will not always be clear, especially to those coming new to the job, just what the right questions might be. In particular, what are the areas in which decision-makers require information? In some few cases, the decision-makers themselves will be clear about this, and the evaluator can (in part, at least) work to a specification. In other circumstances, the evaluator would benefit by having a reasonably specific notion of what he should be looking at. There would seem to be certain logical areas about which information will be needed (if it is not already available from other sources). First, the decision-maker needs to know if the programme is *feasible*; it is no use wasting time pursuing an idea which no one, in any circumstances, can use. Secondly, he will need to know about the *effectiveness* of the programme along a number of dimensions. To be both fair and honest, these dimensions will need to include those which the developer of the programme thinks are important, and also those seen as important by other people (including anyone opposed to the programme). Effectiveness might ideally include not only a study of the particular programme, but also a comparison of techniques etc. used in the programme with others that could have been used. Thirdly (but by no means least important), the decision-maker will need evidence from which he can decide, in the end, whether he feels that the programme has *educational value* for the students with whom he is concerned.

Another factor which may help to determine which questions should be asked is the point in the life of the project or programme at which the evaluation is being undertaken. Scriven (1967) used the terms *formative* and *summative* to refer respectively to evaluation mainly intended to help form the new curriculum, and evaluation designed to give a final judgement on a finished programme. In these terms, evaluations in Britain have been almost exclusively formative. Some exceptions have been the evaluation of the initial teaching alphabet by Warburton and Southgate (1969), the study of French in the primary school by Burstall et al. (1974), and Reid's evaluation of *Breakthrough to Literacy* (1975).

It may be wondered whether this stark division is helpful. Even an evaluation which concentrates on the revision of the programme concurrently with its development, such as Harlen's (1975), is bound to have a great deal in it to help anyone making a summative judgement on the adoption of the curriculum. A cluster analysis was carried out on conditions in those schools associated in the trials with successful running of the Science 5–13 programme; the resulting information may be used by, for instance, local education authority (LEA) science advisers in deciding whether to recommend particular schools to adopt Science 5–13. In a similar way, an evaluation which is avowedly summative, such as Reid's (1975) work on *Breakthrough to Literacy*, does in fact make points which, had they been made at the trials stage, would have led to a revision of the curriculum. Since they are made after publication, these points (such as the need for teachers to pay particular attention to the way in which the slower learners use the materials, and the fact that most of the pupils did not have instruction about the actual mechanics of hand-writing) will, if given sufficient publicity, be valuable to teachers in revising the way in which they use *Breakthrough*. Indeed, the whole notion of a dichotomy between summative and formative evaluation would seem to ignore the possibility of any attempt by the users to develop the programme further. While this possibility exists, no evaluation can be truly summative.

At the same time, it is often useful to know the stage in the programme's life at which the evaluation was undertaken; certain sorts of interaction or experience occur only during a development phase, for instance, and an evaluation carried out after the development had stopped could have no reliable means of observing them. In order to preserve this distinction, and convey useful information to readers of evaluation reports, perhaps the use of the terms *concurrent evaluation* and *subsequent evaluation* would be helpful. The confusion of the purposes of evaluation in relation to the developer and possible users has serious consequences when it leads evaluators to think that, because they are engaged in concurrent evaluation, they are responsible only to the developer. The result can be that reports of the evaluation will be available only to the developer, and that information which would undoubtedly have value for a potential user will not become public knowledge.

One particular way in which a concurrent evaluation can have much wider application is the use of the evaluation situation to try to add to our total understanding of the process of teaching in general, and of curriculum development in particular. Cronbach, notably, has issued a clear challenge to evaluators (1963, p. 675): 'Hopefully, evaluation studies will go beyond reporting on this or that course and help us to understand educational learning. Such insight will, in the end, contribute to the development of all courses rather than just the course under test'. Clearly, this suggestion raises problems. An evaluation is (usually) concerned with a single set of trials of a single curriculum (see definition of 'curriculum', p. 3). How can results from this single case be generalized? The answer is that they cannot, but the evaluation situation can be used both to construct hypotheses about learning, and to test other people's hypotheses. Nor do these hypotheses need to be generated from a single instance; although at one level the evaluation deals with a single curriculum, at another level it has as many different cases as there are trial schools, or teachers, or even pupils. In any case, the construction of a hypothesis goes beyond one statistically significant result. It is an attempt to suggest possible relationships between the variables in a situation;

its purpose is to make it easier for the next worker to develop the ideas by using the new evaluation study as an opportunity for testing, and revising, the hypothesis. If the hypothesis is truly grounded in the data, then it is highly likely to be relevant to other situations—even though it is only by chance that an early hypothesis would survive repeated application to other evaluation situations. (An important rationale and methodology for developing theory in such situations can be found in Glaser and Strauss, 1967.) As Westbury (1970, p. 257) put it: 'theory must inform the deliberation that is evaluation, but at the same time it must grow from deliberation'.

Some writers would see this aspect of evaluation—the attempt to work towards a theory of teaching and learning that will help us to understand our observations—as absolutely vital. There are others who feel that it is not necessary, like Glass and Worthen (1972, p. 83):

There is considerable debate among investigators in education about the extent to which evaluators should explain ('understand') the phenomena they evaluate. We do not view explanations as the goal of evaluation. A fully proper and useful evaluation can be conducted without explaining *why* the product or program being evaluated is good or bad, or *how* it produces its effects. This is fortunate, since evaluation in education is so needed, and credible explanations of educational phenomena are so rare.

Indeed, many may feel that the quest for 'understanding' blurs the distinction between evaluation and research. This distinction is not an idle one; the way in which a task is perceived will delineate certain ways of going about it. It is likely that any educational task will be approached in one way if it is seen as evaluation, and quite another if it is seen as research.

What, then, are these differences between research and evaluation? One major distinction can be made along a dimension of relative dependence or independence. It is possible to imagine the research worker creating his own terms of reference, setting up his own research problem, and perhaps even manufacturing his own research situation; evaluators will rarely have any of these opportunities, and can never have the last. For evaluation to take place, there must be some *other* activity (either before or at the same time) to evaluate. The purpose of the evaluation (whichever definition is adopted) is to obtain data about the other activity. This service function of evaluation has important consequences for the responsibility of the evaluator as opposed to the researcher. It is usually accepted (and is indeed a canon of academic freedom) that the researcher's main responsibility is either towards the academic community as a whole, or to some supreme value like 'truth' or 'science'. While it is to be hoped that the evaluator feels this higher responsibility too, he must also recognize that he has a major commitment to the programme and to the people concerned with it—the development team, teachers, parents, children and those with the task of spending public money. Among the questions which the evaluator will have to face, is that of the utility of the programme. As Glass and Worthen (1972, p. 84) put it: 'A touch-stone for discriminating an evaluator and a researcher is to ask whether the inquiry would be regarded as a failure if it produced no information on whether the phenomenon studied was useful or useless. A research answer *qua* researcher will probably say "No".'

Is there, then, any difference in the methods and techniques used by evaluators and researchers ? If this is asking whether evaluators and researchers have the same goals of objectivity, reliability and validity in collecting their data, then clearly there must be no difference. If the question is about how far evaluation need follow what have, up to now, been accepted as good educational research methods, then there will be a different answer. The Phi Delta Kappa National Study Committee on Evaluation (Stufflebeam et al., 1971) spends some time arguing that it is entirely inappropriate for evaluation to try to follow the rigid model of the educational (or, more accurately, psychological) experiment. Other authors have suggested that, given the particular decision needs of evaluation, even such generally accepted norms as the level at which an effect is taken to be statistically significant could be relaxed. There now seems to be a growing tendency (crystallized by Parlett and Hamilton in Chapter 5) to suggest that the evaluator abandon the traditional experimental model altogether, and seek his methodology from fields such as social anthropology, or the participant observation tradition in sociology.

Another way of seeing the relationship between evaluation and other sorts of educational research has been suggested by Cronbach and Suppes (1969) in their exploration of the idea of 'disciplined inquiry'. This is the process of investigating a problem using the methods and questions which have been developed by scholars in particular disciplines. 'Disciplined inquiry has a quality that distinguishes it from other sources of opinion and belief. The disciplined inquiry is conducted and reported in such a way that the argument can be painstakingly examined'. It will not necessarily follow well-established, formal procedures, but it will set out the evidence, some estimate of its reliability, and the steps followed in arriving at conclusions. Cronbach and Suppes further suggest that disciplined inquiry in education can be seen as either *conclusion-oriented* or *decision-oriented*, depending on the origins and aims of the work and, in particular, on the freedom of the investigator to redefine his task as he goes along. From what has been said about the service nature of curriculum evaluation, this would seem to be a prime example of decision-oriented inquiry; but it is also clear that, like all other educational research activities, evaluation should be based on procedures which are as disciplined as those used in the tightest psychological experiment, even though the procedures need not be the same in both cases.

It might be useful to conclude by realizing what evaluation *cannot* do. One of the most thought-provoking papers an evaluator can read is that by Flynn

(1972), which makes the devastatingly simple point that an evaluation can only consider evidence of what is or what has been—not of what might be. An evaluation of an educational programme, for instance, can examine how the basic idea has been interpreted by the development team and how this interpretation has been developed in the school situation. It can show what effects the development programme has had for a wide range of participants; it can even recommend whether this development should be adopted in the schools. But what an evaluation can *never* do is to pronounce authoritatively on future developments, or on what effects the basic idea might have if it were developed in a different way. This has very important implications for the way in which evaluations are used. It may be reasonable for decisions to be taken, on the basis of evaluation evidence, about the adoption or discontinuance of a particular form of development. But evaluation evidence from a study of work in the field cannot validly be used to discredit the ideas behind the development. This evaluation will not point up the *potential* of an idea— the decision must be taken on quite other grounds. Evaluation will not make our difficult decisions for us; it is a servant, not a master.

Conclusions and summary

Curriculum evaluation should not be confused with the skill of making informed judgements, nor with the assessment and testing of pupils. While there may be elements of both of these in the total process, it is more useful in complex areas of educational decision (which necessarily raise issues of public concern) if the collection of information and the making of decisions are seen as separate acts. A definition of evaluation based solely on measuring the achievement of pre-specified objectives is unlikely to give us evidence about a wide enough range of factors for us to see *why* something is happening— though this is usually what we wish to know. Nor is it likely to be able to help us build up a more complete picture of education. Evaluation provides a considerable opportunity for both the development and the testing of hypotheses about learning and about change. On the other hand, curriculum evaluation will not make our difficult decisions for us; information about what *is* or what *has been* is not the sole and infallible guide to what *might be*.

A working definition of evaluation must retain flexibility and scope for the evaluator and the decision-maker, while at the same time helping those using it to come to grips straight away with the main problems. A useful formulation might be:

Curriculum evaluation is the collection and provision of evidence, on the basis of which decisions can be taken about the feasibility, effectiveness and educational value of curricula.

2 Evaluation—information for decision-makers

David Tawney

The evaluator has the task of providing information about a curriculum project on which different groups of people—from the project team to parents and administrators—will base educational decisions. How should he interact with these groups, and what is the nature of decision-making, particularly in an educational context? Who are the decision-makers at the different stages in the life of a project—planning, trials and revision, dissemination, adoption? What information do they need, and from what source? Finally, at what point does the evaluator himself distinguish between the decisions necessarily involved in his task and those primary decisions that properly belong to others?

INTRODUCTION

'One group of teachers in that school wants to introduce engineering science A level, another Nuffield physics, but their sixth form is far too small for both. How shall I advise them?'   (Science adviser)

'What strategy shall I suggest that this LEA adopt to disseminate my project?'   (Project director)

'If we have too many photographs in the guide, it is going to put the cost up. Find out what the trial teachers think about them.'
                                                    (Project team member)

'We hear a lot about publications and meetings but little about what is going on in the classroom. Can we find out what the children are doing?'   (Member of staff of a funding agency)

These fictitious questions echo many the author has heard in the context of curriculum development. All are demands for information and all imply that decisions have to be made on the basis of this information. If it is accepted, following the arguments of Chapter 1, that evaluation is the provision of information for decision-makers, then it is the task of the evaluator to try to meet these demands.

There are many groups of decision-makers: project team members, teachers, parents, LEA administrators including subject advisers, consultative committee members, the funding agency, publishers and last, but by no means least important, pupils. All may need to make decisions about a curriculum development and so all may need to be provided with information, which is not the same as data, as Stufflebeam et al. (1971, p. 41) point out. Data convey information only if they reduce uncertainty. Both the form and the nature of the information required will vary with the kind of decision to be made— the nature because different decisions require different selections of information, and the form because different decisions are made by different groups of decision-makers with different backgrounds and expectations.

To inform, rather than just present data, an evaluator has to interact with the decision-maker. He must explore some of the constraints on the situation in which a decision has to be made, the options open to the decision-maker, his other sources of information, his values and expectations. Before the evaluator can inform he will need to ask questions. His relationship with the different decision-makers he may serve takes many forms; obviously, an evaluator engaged in a formative study can have close contact with his principal audience—the project team—while one producing a summative report is unlikely even to meet most of the potential adopters whose decisions he is hoping to inform. However, even if discussion is restricted to formative evaluation, there can be a wide range of situations: at one extreme the evaluation may be funded separately and based apart from the project, as with Project Technology (Tawney, 1973); at the other, despite a strong commitment of the project to evaluation, no person is appointed to act solely as evaluator. Such was the policy of the Nuffield Advanced Biological Science Project, which adopted a strategy requiring different members of the project team to assume evaluation roles at different times, and which made considerable use of outside experts and those co-ordinating trials.

The advantages of the first, independent arrangement are that an evaluation study is more likely to be conducted seriously if someone is given a specific responsibility for it; further, that information is more freely given to persons whose independence ensures confidentiality; lastly, that information from an independent source is more credible. The advantages of having no separate evaluator are that this facilitates the blending of 'the work of developers and evaluators, allowing their separate expertise and motivation to be expressed without polarizing into a position of antagonism' (Kelly, 1973a, p. 93); also, there is little doubt that an evaluator who turns his hand for a short time to development work gains credibility in the eyes of the developers. There is no ideal strategy of evaluation; many factors need to be considered when planning an evaluation, and the position of the evaluator and the distribution of evaluation roles need to be negotiated in each case.

No matter what overall strategy is adopted, this author believes that, when a decision has to be made, someone must stand apart, disengage himself from the process of judgement and adopt the evaluation role of presenting information, clarifying value positions and seeing that all options are considered. In some cases, such a 'neutral chairman' role may well be assumed by the project director himself, but in any case he who has collected the information should try to avoid participating in the decision. He may present other people's judgements but he ought not to judge the main issues himself. The judgement he himself exercises is at the level of choosing data and deciding how to collect and present them. Since even these choices cannot be value-free, he must declare his own values. However, this freedom from making judgements is again a matter for negotiation; it is open to an administrator commissioning an evaluation study to insist that the evaluator judge for him.

In this chapter, evaluation has been treated as the work of one man, called the evaluator, who executes all the evaluation tasks discussed. This policy has been adopted, at the risk of appearing to exalt the position of evaluator, to achieve simplicity in writing and is not intended to favour a particular evaluation strategy.

DECISION-MAKING

The task of the evaluator in providing the decision-maker with information, rather than just data, and in avoiding taking his decisions for him, is made harder because we lack understanding of the decision-making process. Decision-making is not, of course, confined to education and has in fact received much attention in the fields of government, business and the armed services; the need for formal training in, and research into, management (including decision-making skills) in the field of education has only recently been perceived. Even in these other fields, the decision-making process is poorly understood. However, there is no doubt that the process is complex and far from rational and open. In a society whose members hold a wide range of value positions, a decision-maker frequently has to take a variety of considerations into account, but it is usually more comfortable to make decisions when these are only half-exposed than when they are brought out into the open, their implications explored, and the pros and cons of the various courses of action stated clearly. Making a decision by 'hunch' has great attractions for the decision-maker, particularly in the educational field where, far from being given a set of clear aims to direct him, he is likely to be accountable to a variety of different groups with different expectations. A headteacher wishing to introduce a curriculum change has to consider his staff, his pupils, their parents, local employers, more advanced educational establishments, the LEA, HM inspectors—a whole range of groups, none of which is likely to hold a unanimous view. In such a situation, the decision-maker meets a strong temptation to push out of his consciousness the need for a decision and to let it 'just happen'.

Fortunately, many decision-makers are experts at semi-rational decision-making, balancing opposing viewpoints as if by instinct and arriving at wise decisions from shrewd assessments apparently based on very little information; this process Stufflebeam et al. (1971, p. 16) call 'shooting from the hip'. However, many decision-makers are not so successful, and it is doubtful if this is the appropriate method in the field of innovation; it is probably most effective in a long-established, slowly changing system in which the decision-maker can follow up his original decision with others, minor adjustments to make it work. The strategy is most dangerous when used in the context of a temporary body set up to produce change in a permanent system. Such a task force can delude itself in many ways and, although too much unfavourable information can lower its morale, it is probably better for it to start with modest expectations and work overtly and rationally towards them than to have to protect itself from recognizing the failures of its high ideals. Some failure must be expected and used fruitfully.

A curriculum development project team is such a task force, a temporary body interacting with a massive and well-established system with strong mechanisms intended to maintain the *status quo*. It is the evaluator's task to help decision-making to be as rational and open as possible; to do this he must provide information and help the decision-makers explore both their own value positions and the options open to them. This concept of decision-making is expressed by Fig. 1, taken from Stufflebeam et al. (1971). The three arrows leading into the 'decision-maker' (who may of course, be more than one person) indicate the services the evaluator might perform: providing information, exploring the options open and clarifying the values of those involved in the decision-making. The arrows leading away from the 'decision-maker' indicate the anticipated outcomes.

DECISIONS, DECISION-MAKERS AND THE INFORMATION THEY REQUIRE DURING A PROJECT'S LIFE CYCLE

In this section, the simple model of decision-making and evaluation described in the introduction will be applied at different points in the life cycle of a project. In each case the decision-makers will be identified and the nature of the decisions examined, in order to suggest possible methods of evaluation. The danger of this approach is that it encourages the view that a project goes through a simple series of stages. This is not the case: there is considerable overlap between the stages mentioned here, and within the overall cycle is a series of smaller cycles, each of which may involve these stages. For example, the decisions taken by a teacher in the adoption phase of a project have often been anticipated by a teacher invited to take part in trials. However, some simplification is necessary.

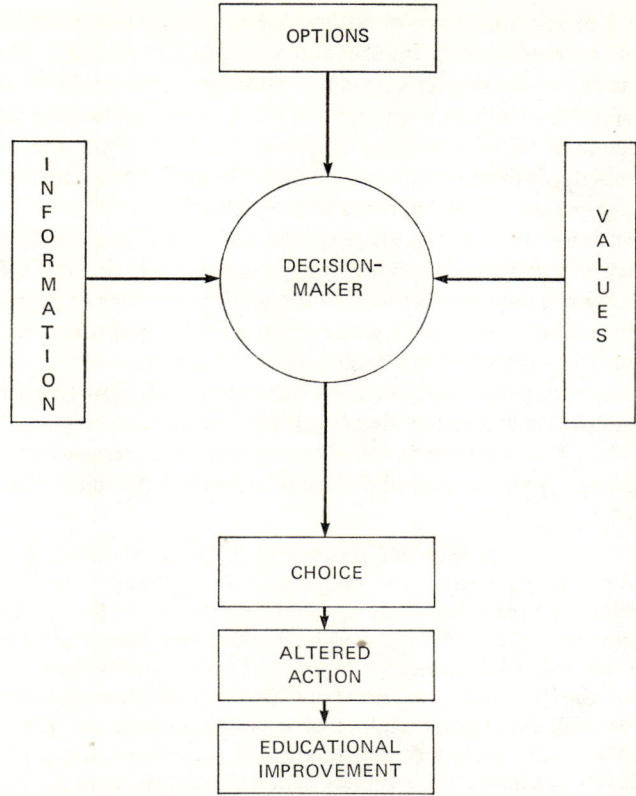

Fig. 1 The evaluator's services for decision-makers (*source:* Stufflebeam et al., 1971, p. 39)

Planning

An evaluator is lucky to be appointed at the start of the project, just after it has been funded. So strong is the view that his job is to measure outcomes that his appointment is frequently deferred until it is hoped that there will be some outcomes for him to measure. However, even if he is appointed at the beginning, some important decisions will already have been made. Aims and an overall strategy will have been outlined in the proposal to the funding body, a director and other staff appointed and, most important, a decision to set up the project taken. The evaluator may well find that the proposal was supported by information collected by the director or by another body; for example, the Nuffield Secondary Science Project made use of Schools Council Working Paper 1, *Science for the Young School Leaver* (1965).

Despite the decisions already taken and the information already gathered, the evaluator has a vital role to play at the planning stage. The aims of the project and its methods have to be decided in greater detail, and to do this openly and rationally much information needs to be collected. The aims of potential users of the project's products must be found, and also the conditions in which they will be used and the whole range of possible activities in the classroom by which the aims might be achieved. Then the strategy of development needs to be considered: should it be based on a centre–periphery, or periphery–periphery model, for example (Schon, 1971)?

The decision-makers at this stage will be the project team with the project consultative committee. It is sometimes prudent to invite the staff of the funding body to play a part in major decisions, and a wise director may well think it important to involve a wider group of potential users, such as trial teachers, and 'significant others' such as HM inspectors.

As has been stated earlier, Nuffield Advanced Biological Science decided not to employ 'an evaluator simply as an external observer and analyst' (Kelly, 1973a, p. 93) but to include an evaluation strategy within the total project strategy, a policy exemplified by the team's approach to this planning stage (p. 94):

A review of current and possible future trends in the biological sciences and their importance to education was undertaken; in addition, a series of working parties including members of the development team, subject specialists and teachers were set up. Most of the working parties were concerned with specific topics, for example, applied biology. They worked out the objectives in teaching these topics, the basic concepts underlying the topics, outline teaching schemes, connections with other topics, types of curriculum materials that might be used, and the type of trials and evaluation required. Some working parties were not specifically concerned with subject content and dealt with matters such as project work and examinations. Meetings were also held with people from the Association for Science Education, colleges and university departments of education, colleges of advanced technology (as they were in 1965), medical and dental schools, industrial organizations, as well as with university biologists to gain some insight into their views of the shape sixth form biology should take. In addition, the project co-operated with a survey conducted by the Royal Society/Institute of Biology's Biological Education Committee, covering some relevant aspects of biology teaching in sixth forms including teachers' opinions about its requirements, analyses of the backgrounds, ability and aspirations of students taking A level biology, the suitability of facilities, and the probable effects of changes in the curriculum.

The data obtained from these sources were presented independently to meetings of the project's development team and consultative committee. Verbatim minutes of these meetings provided further data and the whole was then analysed by the project organizer; a document, intended to represent a consensus of their judgement, with a draft statement of objectives and an outline scheme of the content, activities and materials to be developed, was presented to the development team separately and then jointly with the consultative committee. At the same time, feedback on it was sought from members of the various working parties. The document was modified and the development team approved a statement of objectives some eleven months after the project commenced.

This passage implies a whole range of information-gathering activities: literature searches, working parties, meetings with interested parties, surveys using questionnaires. Of particular note are the 'verbatim minutes' of project team and consultative committee meetings; these are invaluable for helping to clarify the value positions of members of these important decision-making bodies, and to identify the options open to them. An evaluator might well want to support these methods by interviewing the decision-makers and recording the interviews on tape. The need for this information would emerge from a study of his other data.

Another notable feature of this passage is the method used to obtain a consensus of the variety of views expressed; techniques for achieving this necessary balance are described in texts on management studies (e.g. Forehand, 1970) but this project used the simple but effective one of referring the first consensus document back to the various working parties and committees for their comments.

So extensive is the evaluation activity in this phase of a project that most members of the project team will be involved in it. The role of the permanent evaluator, if there is one, may well be to monitor this activity and himself concentrate on organizing and collating information and articulating value positions. It could also be his responsibility to make comments such as: 'Your intention to do such-and-such seems to have evaporated. Are you clear why?' and 'We seem to be adopting this policy because it is being advocated by this powerful group. Is that the only reason?'

Lastly, it must be emphasized that, despite the likelihood and indeed desirability that the aims of a project will be modified during its life, some decisions reached in this area are far-reaching and difficult to reverse. The project director and his fellow developers may well have started work with very definite ideas on the aims of the project and the contingent methods; they were probably appointed to the project because they were already creatively involved in development work, albeit on a small scale. The greater the initial commitment to a set of aims and methods, the more important it is that someone should adopt the evaluative role of encouraging their exploration, as well as examining the value position behind them and considering alternatives.

Part of the information gathered by Nuffield Advanced Biological Science in the initial phase was not concerned directly with the aims of the project, the contents of the course, the abilities to be developed and the methods to be used, but with the conditions in which the classes using the project would be operating. Another evaluation study which attached great importance to collecting information in this area was that of Kaner for the Mathematics for the Majority Project, where a major objective was to provide material for non-specialists teaching mathematics to older secondary children of average and below-average ability. The evaluator decided that little was known about these teachers (Kaner, 1973, p. 132) 'How many such teachers were in action; what were their specialities; what help did they need most urgently?' A survey of 100 schools drawn at random from the *Education Authorities Directory* revealed some significant information, including the statistic that over half the below-average pupils were taught mathematics by non-specialist teachers whose own specialisms ranged from geography to religious instruction. Such information was vitally relevant to the project and must have caused the project team to question its decision to provide only teachers' guides, leaving the teachers themselves to produce pupil worksheets.

The early curriculum projects in the United Kingdom do not seem to have seen the need to question strategies of innovation; for example, the centre–periphery model, in which a central team devises materials and methods to be tried out by trial schools, appears to have been readily accepted. A project starting today has a wider range of models from which to choose, and it is an important evaluation task to ensure that the project team and the project consultative committee consider a range of strategies before reaching a decision to adopt one of them. It may not be appropriate that the evaluator himself adopt the neutral evaluation role in the discussion leading to a decision on overall strategy. He may find himself in the role of advocate, pleading for the strategy to take account of the need for evaluation, and contain sufficient flexibility to respond to its findings. For example, the evaluator may view the choice of the number of trial schools and the lengths of the trial periods differently from those who are developing materials.

Trials and revision

At this phase of a project, decisions usually relate to detailed choices of content and method. Much depends, of course, on the nature of the project: in some, much more fundamental decisions may be needed. Many decisions will be made about trial schools—their selection, communication with them, and their support; others may have to be made about examinations. The decision-makers will include the project team, the project consultative committee and the funding body. LEA officials and trial teachers will also have important decisions to make, and they may be joined later by publishers and equipment manufacturers. If the project is developing a course leading to a public examination, the examining boards and institutions of higher education too will play a vital part.

Most of the project team will spend most of their time during this phase in producing and revising materials and methods, and suggesting to teachers how they might be used. They may well spend some time on evaluation activities, particularly in a project with an overall evaluation strategy like Nuffield Advanced Biological Science. Nevertheless, the role of the evaluator is likely to become more clearly defined and his tasks more differentiated. He will need to find out much more about the trial schools. Frequently, a project has little choice of schools and may have to select almost all those whose names have been put forward by an LEA or which have themselves volunteered. There are several important considerations in selection. The schools need to be grouped together for ease of servicing and mutual comfort during trials but the groups need to be widely distributed to help dissemination after the project is finished. The evaluator will be concerned that the samples of pupils and of schools are large enough to enable some generalizations to be drawn from trial results, both about the methods and materials of the project and about any assessment procedures. Hopefully, the sample will reflect the national pattern in type of school and in pupil ability.

The trial schools may well have to be selected in haste. The evaluator in comparative leisure must find out more about them, probably using postal questionnaires or checklists completed by visiting project team members or local helpers; a wide range of information is needed. Kelly (1971b, p. 315) found that 'the standards of the A-level performance of previous students in the [sample] schools and of the students in the trials at O-level were slightly higher in some respects than that of the equivalent national population'. Had they been very different, his team might well have decided to modify the sample at the next phase of the trials. Even if this could not have been done, the knowledge would be of great importance when texts were revised, the findings from different elements of the sample being weighted, perhaps informally, to obtain a product to suit the national population.

Teacher characteristics are also informative. Tawney (1973) and Gunn found that the success of the Project Technology *Photocell Applications* material in a school depended strongly on the trial teachers' previous experience in electronics. Teachers' opinions on the importance of aims and on the likelihood of their being achieved are also useful, as Kelly showed (1972a, 1973a). The Project Technology evaluation unit (Tawney, Swinswood and Gunn, 1973) continually found that teachers had only vague ideas as to what educational outcomes they could expect using Project Technology materials; this finding too was relevant to decisions made during the revision of materials and to the training of teachers during both trials and dissemination.

One of the most comprehensive pictures of the trial situation was obtained by Harlen (1975), using information obtained from questionnaires and checklists. This was analysed by computer, using a program for classifying qualitative data by cluster analysis. She was able to relate the responses of teachers, made to questions concerned with the Science 5–13 course units, to the learning environments of their classes; for example, a preference for 'more suggestions in less detail' concerning activities in the unit *Working with Wood* (p. 44) was positively and quite strongly associated with teachers whose classes were accustomed to active discovery methods, with desks arranged in irregular groups, working a fully integrated timetable, and who appreciated the meaning of the project objectives and approved of them. This information was invaluable when decisions were taken on how to revise the material to suit teachers' requirements; even more useful were the comments of teachers at the other end of the spectrum—those unaccustomed to discovery methods and informal classroom arrangements.

The Humanities Curriculum Project was developing a method of teaching rather than a set of materials, so that the decisions which had to be made on the basis of information obtained from trials were of a different kind. Mac-Donald (1973, p. 84) refers to the information obtained shortly after the commencement of the first trials: 'The immediate impact of the project was on the whole alarming. There was enormous confusion and misunderstanding, leading to a general failure on the part of the schools to respond appropriately to the project specifications.' Some of the elements of the confusion to which MacDonald refers were the project team's under-estimation of the headmaster's importance in this type of innovation, of the strength of a tradition of teacher dominance and custodial attitudes, and of the difficulties of effective communication. This information led to important changes in communication and support strategies rather than in the materials.

Other sources of information valuable for decision-making in the area of revision are attainment studies. In the constraints imposed by a curriculum development project, the small samples and the limited time available, it is difficult to get statistically reliable results from the classical design of pre- and post-testing, experimental and control groups, and not usually worth the effort. Nevertheless, attainment testing can be valuable, the relative scores for different parts of a course indicating areas where attention is needed. The Project Technology evaluation unit spent some time devising tests of creativity and problem-solving ability for use in a study of the *Control Technology* course (Dennien et al., 1973); they found it impossible to draw any statistically sound conclusions but were nevertheless able to use their data to support other evidence suggesting, for example, that without important changes in teaching strategy, there was unlikely to be any transfer of any problem-solving ability developed in the context of *Control Technology* to wider areas.

In a curriculum development project involving a public examination, regular pupil assessment is expected and provides the evaluator with valuable information. The Nuffield Science Teaching Projects at both O and A level had to provide trial examinations—not only terminal ones on which GCEs would be awarded but yearly examinations and 'mocks'; the purpose of these, besides providing assessments of individual pupils, was to point to any deficiencies in the course, at the same time reassuring both teachers and their classes that they were making satisfactory general progress. These tests and examinations, because they are part of the school scene and expected by both pupils and teachers, form a 'natural' means of evaluation and, quite apart from providing information on the relative attainability of objectives and on examination techniques, serve to provoke discussions at which these objectives are clarified and value positions revealed. Sometimes this natural means of evaluation can be extended: Kelly (1971b) was able to use an S level paper to compare the achievements of some pupils who had followed the Nuffield Advanced Biological Science course with those of followers of more traditional courses; he concluded that the Nuffield pupils were achieving the objectives tested by this common paper at least as well as the other pupils.

In the trials of a project involving an examination, the examination itself is under trial and certain to be revised during the life of the project. The *Control Technology* course developed by Project Technology formed the basis of courses leading to CSE Mode 3 examinations of five different boards. The evaluation unit (Tawney, Swinswood and Gunn, 1973) analysed the questions appearing in the examination papers and produced profiles of each paper, showing the weightings apparently given to each of the objectives tested. The unit was concerned not that there should be conformity with the objectives of the original course but that any departures should be made consciously. Its findings were intended to guide the revision of those parts of the course material which dealt with the objectives of the course, with the making of submissions to GCE examining boards and with assessment techniques; they should also help in the revision of the examinations already established.

Attempts to assess changes in pupil attitudes which can be attributed to participation in a course have been made by several evaluators. The Project Technology evaluation unit (Dennien et al., 1973) used a modified version of Meyer's *A Test of Interests* while Alexander (1974) used the National Foundation for Educational Research's *Pupil Opinion Poll*; Harlen (1975) devised a most ingenious attitude scale suitable for young children. However, in all these cases the comparisons of pre- and post-applications were disappointing: instead of gains being recorded, attitudes appeared, on the contrary, to have deteriorated, and the most that could be said of the trial groups was that the deterioration was less than that of the control groups. This effect has been observed in other studies on science courses, for example that of Laughton and Wilkinson (1968). The Humanities Curriculum Project, on the other hand (Hamingson, 1973), was able to show stable gains in some of the attitude measures used by its evaluators. In view of the difficulties associated with the formal measurement of attitudes, it is not surprising that most projects have relied on less formal methods, such as discussion and questionnaires, to obtain pupils' views.

A fourth source of data, which yields valuable information for decisions concerned with revising materials and methods and communicating with teachers, is provided by studies of classroom transactions and processes.

Direct observation is very time-consuming and so curriculum projects have made little use of it, but it can provide information which is important, frequently unexpected and obtainable in no other way. For example, a recent study carried out by Southgate and Lewis (1973) showed that a relatively small proportion of the time primary school children spend learning to read involves contact with the materials of reading schemes. This is a vitally important piece of information at a time when there is much debate about the relative merits of rival schemes.

The evaluation study of Nuffield Secondary Science carried out by Alexander (1974) used a simple schedule administered by ten observers to one or two classes each; each observer recorded nine to ten lesson for each class. Observers were required to record which one of twelve activities predominated in each five-minute interval and to rate pupil participation on a 1–5 scale. The study was begun too late to have much formative influence; this is regrettable because it produced information which would have been valuable in modifying the advice given in the *Teachers' Guide* on the design of workcards, on choice of routes through the materials, and on the adaptation of teaching styles to different levels of pupil ability.

It is largely because of its time-consuming nature that such structured observation, although valuable, has hitherto been little used for evaluation in the UK. Many projects have used less regular and less structured observation. The Science 5–13 Project, for example, used as observers team members and local project organizers (local advisers or teachers); these completed a report form after each period of observation (Harlen, 1975). As well as providing vital information for decisions concerned with revision, such visits made primarily for the purpose of observation form a means of communicating with trial schools and of providing the encouragement needed to help counter the difficulties which any new course provides. The Project Technology evaluation unit (Tawney, Swinswood and Gunn, 1973) continually found that the trial schools wanted the support of more visits from the project team and the evaluation unit.

Information can be obtained from trials through the use of checklists completed from interviews with trial teachers and from questionnaires. The Project Technology evaluation unit, which was faced with the need to obtain information from the trials of thirteen very different sets of materials, made considerable use of these and obtained a good deal of data useful for both revision of materials and the future conduct of trials. For example, questionnaires showed that a large proportion of teachers felt that the project's pack of workcards intended to stimulate project work (*Project Briefs*) required more cards suitable for the lower ability groups, a finding obviously relevant to decisions concerned with the final selection of materials for publishing.

Harlen (1975, p. 86) described how, in Science 5–13:

Undoubtedly the most positive aid to revising the trial units came from the teachers' questionnaires; here were the reports of how far the suggestions could be put into practice, the accounts of how activities had begun and ended, reasons for parts of a unit being unsatisfactory, and suggestions for changes. No other source of information was so rich in detailed and definite indications of how the material could be made more helpful to teachers.

However, she continues by stating how necessary it was to supplement this information with contextual data obtained by other means.

As was mentioned earlier, Kelly (1972a, 1973a) gained some interesting data through questionnaires on trial teachers' views on the desirability and attainability of pupil and course objectives. As this led to a study which illustrates well the formative role of evaluation in the trials phase, it will be discussed in more detail here. Teachers were asked to rate a list of objectives for the extent they thought that these were desirable and attainable both at the start of the trials and towards the end. Results showed that the ratings of desirability made on these two occasions were very similar but that ratings for attainability varied, reflecting the relative successes of different parts of the course. For instance, the development of one ability, 'handling quantitative information and assessing the error and degree of significance involved' (1972a, p. 29), was considered highly desirable in both ratings but at the start of the trials only a minority thought that it could be achieved. At the end of the trials, the rating for its achievability was almost as high as for its desirability. How was this change brought about?

The initial scepticism of trial teachers that this objective could be achieved was at first supported by the low facilities of items devised to test it in termly examinations and by teachers' ratings of its achievement. Discussions with teachers at area meetings and with others yielded the views that this lack of success was due both to the low mathematical ability of the pupils and to the difficulty of the mathematics included in the course. To test the first view, the O level results in mathematics and biology of pupils at some of the trial schools were compared with those of pupils at the same schools studying physical sciences and mathematics. This showed that, despite the presence of a substantial minority of students with poor results, 72 per cent of the biologists had an acceptable background in mathematics. The poor opinion that teachers held of their pupils' mathematical ability could be attributed to the low correlation between O level biology and mathematics grades and the low number of very mathematically able students taking biology. 'These influences appear to have disguised the fact that the great majority of students had a reasonable O level background in mathematics' (1973a, p. 105).

After an analysis of the mathematics content in the course had shown that it should have been within the grasp of this substantial majority, the problem was discussed by groups of teachers at a national conference, who concluded that it was caused by the learning strategies involved; they made recommendations to improve them. The advice was followed in the production of work for the second year of trials and much higher achievement resulted.

This study illustrates several important points. It is the result of the evaluator responding not to a need which was anticipated and prescribed in some grand evaluation plan, but to one seen only later; thus it is an example of what is termed 'responsive evaluation' (Stake, 1972). A variety of sources of information was used: GCE results, termly examinations, teachers' ratings of desirability, achievability and achievement, conference discussion. Finally, the group of decision-makers was widened; the ultimate decisions may have been made by the project team but they were based on the recommendations of the trial teachers.

The last sources of information to be described are very informal but nevertheless much used and indeed valuable, particularly if supported with other sources. The first is to invite informal feedback, unstructured comments on the trial material, perhaps on a duplicate copy of teachers' guides, in the margins and on the back of pages. This means was used by several of the Nuffield science projects. Some of the teachers' comments, often quotations of their pupils' remarks, were sufficiently informative to warrant their inclusion in the published texts; all were valuable for revision purposes. Also of very great value are meetings of trial teachers, for these provide opportunity to assess reactions not only to existing practices but also to proposed alterations.

Dissemination

By 'dissemination' is meant the conscious process by which a knowledge and understanding of the developed curriculum project, its materials and ideas, is spread beyond those involved in its development. The decision-makers involved include the project team, the funding agency, publishers, equipment suppliers, inspectors, science advisers and training institutions. Dissemination is an important stage in a curriculum project, the importance of which is being increasingly perceived. Previously, as Kelly (1971a, p. 87) has pointed out, '. . . because curriculum projects are invariably limited in time by funds and resources, the subsequent implementation of their work other than in trial schools has tended to be uncontrolled, variable and inevitably less than was hoped.' In the past, the gulf between the dispersal of the project team and the publication of revised materials proved disastrously uncrossable and dissemination suffered; Nuffield Junior Science is a notable example of a project which failed at this phase (Wastnedge, 1968). Kelly provides a useful structure for a consideration of dissemination and raises a number of issues (1971a), but inevitably he asks more questions than he answers: the process of dissemination is more complex and difficult to control than other parts of the process of innovation.

It is not only a lack of adequate resources which limits dissemination; in the decentralized educational system of England and Wales, teachers are difficult to inform, let alone influence and it is, for example, the Schools Council's policy that, despite its anxiety for its costly products to be accepted by the consumer, he must be allowed to make a free choice. The autonomy of the teacher is sacred.

The planning of the dissemination strategy of a project is an area in which vital decisions are made and, as elsewhere, the evaluator needs to provide information and to help the decision-makers explore the options in the light of this information and their own values. Although the majority of decisions about dissemination will be made towards the end of the trials phase, some need to be made at the planning stage so that dissemination strategy needs to be considered right from the start. It may affect the contracts offered to team members; it should be considered when deciding the location and number of trial schools. Should these be supported by some local group such as a teachers' centre? Or by a regional group structure, such as Project Technology established? This last project attached so much importance to dissemination that it gave high priority to this regional structure, a policy which may have paid dividends in terms of dissemination but caused problems at one time when the project had no materials to distribute to the expectant groups.

How freely should trial material be circulated? The original tight security of Nuffield (O level) Physics caused bad public relations and had to be modified. On the other hand, the wide distribution of trial material invests it with a finality it does not deserve or desire and, so the publishers fear, may reduce sales of the final product. Should there be a newsletter? Consistent with its emphasis on dissemination, Project Technology right from its establishment produced a *Bulletin* distributed free about four times a year to any interested teacher. One of the earliest tasks of the evaluation unit was to carry out a survey of the opinions of readers on certain aspects of this bulletin (Tawney, 1973).

Thus, there are many tactics which can be employed in an overall dissemination strategy, much experience from which information can be gleaned, many decisions to be made. Here again, as in the collection of information needed to form the overall aims of a project, the task may have to be shared by several team members, the evaluator acting as overall counsellor.

During the trials and revision phases of a project, the evaluator has to monitor the dissemination mechanisms being assembled. Is a regional group really working as well as its co-ordinator claims? How effective is the newsletter? Why is the project getting on better in some LEAs than others? The project team will need answers to these questions before the dissemination stage begins and may well expect the evaluator to provide evidence from the field.

As the project reaches the end of the revision stage, existing dissemination mechanisms may have to be speeded up, new ones established. Are corrections to the original strategy required? How can co-operation with colleges and departments of education be strengthened? How can more LEA advisers be involved? Is the original plan to set up a permanent base, as the Nuffield Science Teaching Projects did at Chelsea and Project Technology did at Nottingham, still feasible? What are the publishers doing to disseminate the publications? To answer these questions of strategy, the project team will need to have explored several alternatives, perhaps examining the experience of earlier projects; several team members are likely to be involved in these evaluation activities.

Even the relatively simple decisions involved in planning dissemination conferences must be informed, and the options explored. Too often, such conferences deserve Clegg's (1968, p. 28) accusation that '. . . the trainers try to convey firelighting techniques by themselves using potfilling methods'. Alexander's (1974) study of Nuffield Secondary Science has important implications for teacher training, suggesting that, during such training, ways by which the teacher could trace the links between school science and the outside world should have been explored. The Project Technology evaluation unit (Tawney, Swinswood and Gunn, 1973) showed the need for discussions of the aims of technological work in teachers' courses.

After the materials have been published, most of the project team will have dispersed to take up new posts, although hopefully one or two members will be left to organize the dissemination. It is seldom that funds have allowed the continued appointment of an evaluator, despite the valuable service he could render in monitoring dissemination tactics. A notable study of this stage is being carried out by Kelly (1973b).

Adoption
The significant difference between this area of decision-making and its predecessors is not temporal, for adoption decisions are made at the start of trials and throughout the dissemination phase; it lies in the change in decision-maker from a seller to a buyer. He is the teacher, LEA adviser or teacher trainer, deciding whether to adopt the course or to recommend its adoption. In seeking to inform him, the evaluator, who previously may have been predominantly concerned with advising his project on the effects of its sales techniques, must now shift his direction to ensure that the consumer is adequately and fairly informed. This change in direction does not require the adoption of double standards; providing information for the disseminator and for the adopter are two aspects of the same task, for in the long term it is likely that successful salesmanship depends on satisfied customers, who in turn depend on an accurate specification of the product and comprehensible directions for its use.

Sometimes the curriculum developer has an inflated image of his product. This has led Kaner (1973, p. 145) to see the job of the evaluator as 'establishing the project's true identity—setting up a counter-image to that set up by the project'. Here he is suggesting that potential adopters should be able to examine not only what a project claims for itself but also what its critics say. However it is more satisfactory when a single, balanced description, incorporating both the pros and cons of a project, can be signed by both the project team and the evaluator.

A teacher's decision to adopt a curriculum is the fundamental one for a project; however excellent its product, its work is wasted unless there are buyers. Almost more than any decision in the innovation process, the decision to adopt is a complex one, often involving many people (Kelly, 1971a, p. 89):

[It] may involve an individual teacher, a committee of administrators, or a combination of these, and almost inevitably, students when, for example, they select to take a new type of course. So subtle can the interaction between such a range of contributors be that the point of adoption is not always easily defined. Sometimes, to quote a subject of one of our enquiries, ' . . . it just seemed to happen.'

This complexity produces problems mainly in the area of presentation and communication. The backgrounds and expectations of those involved in the adoption decision vary greatly and so information needs to be presented in different ways: for example, the description of a project designed for an LEA adviser would vary in context, length and form of presentation from one suitable for students. Such descriptions are published in a variety of places, such as teachers' guides, newsletters, publishers' lists and journal articles, and are given orally at conferences and courses. Kelly (1971a) has indicated some of the factors which should be considered in planning effective communication in this area, but there can be no doubt that the most valuable information comes from experience gained in communicating with trial teachers and others early in the life of a project.

The evaluation unit of the Humanities Curriculum Project saw its main task as informing those responsible for adoption decisions and so its first two objectives (MacDonald, 1973, p. 88) were:

(a) to ascertain the effects of the project, document the circumstances in which they occurred, and present this information in a form which would help educational decision-makers to evaluate the likely consequences of adopting the programme;
(b) to describe the existing situation and operations of the schools being studied so that the decision-makers could understand more fully what it was they were trying to change . . .

To obtain the information necessary for this task, the evaluation unit used a range of methods. From a large sample of schools (c. 100), information was obtained from a variety of sources: a battery of instruments used for pre- and post-tests, multiple-choice feedback instruments completed by the teacher and monitored by pupils, semistructured teacher diaries, questionnaires, unstructured judgement data from teachers and pupils. This broad study was complemented by intensive case studies of eleven schools, involving the patterns of decision-making, communication, training and support in their areas, and by a study of the dynamics of discussion by tape, videotape and observation. The problem with such a large study lies in processing the data obtained so that they can be used in time. This project was fortunate in having a funded dissemination phase which both provided, and could be guided by, the information gathered by the evaluation unit. Preliminary findings were rapidly published through an evaluation newsletter and used in dissemination conferences.

CONCLUSION

The previous section makes clear how complex and all-embracing is the evaluator's role if evaluation is seen as the provision of information for decision-makers. Decisions are made everywhere in the life cycle of the project and where there is a decision, there the evaluator has a task. So much information is needed in a project, and so many people need to be involved in data collection besides the official evaluator, that Kelly's view (1973a, p. 93) that it is not an evaluator that a project needs but 'an evaluation strategy within the total project strategy' is attractive.

However, evaluation is more than data collection: as has been said, it involves the processing and presentation of data to turn them into information, the articulation of value positions, the exploration of alternatives. Again, others besides the evaluator will play a part in these processes in any project which has what MacDonald calls an 'evaluation atmosphere'. Yet even in such a project, the evaluator has a role which is both necessary and clearly defined: it is necessary because these processes must be carefully monitored by someone whose prime responsibility is to do so, and it becomes clearly defined when decisions are taken. At this point the evaluator should refuse to participate. After the information has been presented, the standpoints of the decision-makers clarified, the alternatives explored, he must hold his peace.

The evaluator has his own decisions—concerned with data collection, processing and presentation—which he must make and explicate. In addition, there are fundamental decisions, negotiated between the evaluator and the project team, as to the relative importance to be given to the different areas of decision-making. Nevertheless, whatever the overall strategy of evaluation adopted, if the evaluator participates in the primary decision-making of the project, he is liable to compromise his position and destroy the evaluation atmosphere which it is his duty to preserve.

3 Change and development in evaluation strategy

Wynne Harlen

This chapter attempts to trace and illustrate recent changes in
evaluation strategy, and account for the proliferation of new
strategies. Two originally distinct approaches have tended to
converge: on one hand, the inadequacy of the 'measurement of
objectives' approach gave rise to strategies with more emphasis on
qualitative description; on the other hand, criticisms of the traditional
'evaluation by informed opinion' led to strategies in which more
objective judgements are made. Three issues concerned in the choice
of strategy are discussed: the question of scale v. scope, the
argument about goal-based and goal-free evaluation, and the
relative emphasis on process and product.

INTRODUCTION

When curriculum development projects were first set up in the United
Kingdom on a national scale, in the early 1960s, there were few models of
evaluation to follow. Since that time, publications suggesting evaluation
models and strategies have proliferated (Stake, 1967a; Provus, 1969; Stufflebeam, 1969; Alkin, 1970; Parlett and Hamilton, 1972 (see Chapter 5); Scriven,
1972; Kourilsky, 1973) though many may be justly criticized for the narrowness of their empirical basis (Lewy, 1973). Present models lack general appli-
cability and frequently do not fit evaluation of materials or situations which
are different from those in which they were developed. To some extent, then,
the over-provision of possible strategies which now exists brings the same
problems as the scarcity of models ten years ago: the evaluator is still left with
few discernible guidelines to help him decide upon or devise a model which
fits his particular project's materials and the educational setting for which they
are devised.

It was natural that the development teams working in the 1960s should base
their evaluation strategies on what seemed to them to be relevant existing
practice. There were two chief sources of experience, distinctly separate and
leading to two very different views of evaluation. One was the work which
had been done in mental testing and the measurement of achievement. The
use of these test instruments enabled a scientific approach to be applied to

curriculum development; achievement of objectives could be measured in experiments which supposedly controlled non-relevant variables. Such an approach is in line with the view of evaluation (Tyler, 1949, p. 105) as:

. . . essentially the process of determining to what extent the educational objectives are actually being realized by the program of curriculum and instruction. However, since educational objectives are essentially changes in human beings . . . then evaluation is the process for determining the degree to which these changes in behavior are actually taking place.

The other source of experience was the informed judgement which has been used to 'evaluate' teaching methods and materials for very many years. Visits by inspectors and others to schools and colleges and the opinions of experts have played a large part in determining the recommendations of national reports on education, and although recent reports have collected objective data, action has often been based on the judgement of individuals. In the 1960s, evaluation based on the judgement of experienced observers was favoured by those who felt that the products of using curriculum materials were too complex and broadly scattered to be encompassed by prescribed objectives or measured by existing techniques. Since informal classroom observation was accepted as reliable enough for the work of HM inspectors and the members of various advisory committees, it seemed to be an obvious strategy for evaluation of early curriculum innovations. The first projects in mathematics and science supported by the Nuffield Foundation adopted evaluation strategies which depended largely on non-experimental data.

The Nuffield Junior Science Project illustrates the early strategy of 'evaluation by opinion'. In 1964–5 about 200 teachers were involved in trials of the draft teaching materials. The teachers were asked to write reports on their work and some, but not all, were visited by team members. There were no tests for children and only general statements about what children might achieve through the work. The reason for this was expressed by R. W. Crossland (1967, p. 6), who made a study of the project in 1965–6: 'The difficulty is that no-one knows what primary children can do and there would be dangers in setting objectives which might become, needlessly, limits'. Crossland's study, the nearest thing to a summative evaluation of this project, itself used subjective data: 'The evidence for children's achievements was gained by summarising the opinions of teachers and organisers and from my own limited observations of questioning the children' (p. 6).

At the same time, the author of this chapter was carrying out an evaluation of another primary science curriculum project—one which illustrates the 'measurement of achievement' strategy (Harlen, 1967). Children taking part in the trials of materials of the Oxford Primary Science Research Project were tested at the beginning of the trial work and on three other occasions throughout a whole year. There were two experimental groups, with slightly different treatments, and two control groups of children who were all tested on the same occasions. Group tests were constructed of items devised to detect behaviours related to the objectives of the experimental programme and altogether about 1500 children were tested on four occasions. The results showed that the experimental groups were generally achieving the objectives towards which they were working, but differences between trial and control varied from one objective to another and from one class to another. It was not possible from the evaluation to learn anything about the conditions which might promote achievement, or how to improve the parts of the material which had been least successful.

It is not difficult to see the deficiencies in both these strategies for evaluation. One is subjective and unreliable, the findings being highly dependent on the value judgements of the persons observing or commenting on the material; the other is too much restricted to outcomes which can be objectively assessed. The results of using these strategies were unsatisfactory because few practical conclusions or guidelines could be derived from them. Consequently, they have been modified, and the changes have brought them much closer to each other. The purely empirical approach has gradually become less restricted; it has developed to include the detection of unintended as well as intended outcomes, and to gather data about processes as well as products. The original formal strategy has thus changed to include some informal procedures. At the same time there has been a move toward strategies and methods which enable the kinds of information previously gathered by informal and highly subjective means to be gathered more objectively: techniques for classroom observation have been developed, using high- or low-inference schedules, video recording, interaction analysis, and so on, which reduce the dependence of the results on the judgement and bias of the observer. Non-empirical methods of evaluation have also been developed by applying content analysis and other intrinsic evaluation procedures to written materials; these methods establish and make clear the criteria of judgement, and in some cases the judgement can be quantified and checked for reliability.

Before looking in more detail at the nature and course of changes in strategy, it is pertinent to ask why the changes have taken place at all. Why were the simple but neat 'evaluation as measuring achievement of objectives' and the quick and painless 'informal observation' strategies not thought adequate in their different ways? Some general reasons can be suggested, but there must have been others which operated in particular circumstances. It is the main burden of this chapter to show that practical experience of using early strategies, as shown in some of the examples given later, played a very large part, as did argument about what role evaluation should have (Chapter 1), but there may well be a further reason which lies beneath the dissatisfaction with results and the argument. Changing values in education could well have played an important part in bringing dissatisfaction with strategies which were previously thought to be satisfactory. Shifts in value positions produce changes in criteria for decision-making, and therefore different kinds of information have to be supplied to decision-makers. Again two themes can be discerned: one is related to the changing values relating to the aims of education, and the other to the development of a view that education is a process which should be subject to analysis and evaluation rather than operating through intangible insights and mysterious rituals.

Until recently, education has been for most pupils a process of acquiring the same stock of knowledge and the same range of skills as the previous generation. The balance between the aims of education relating to passing on accumulated knowledge and the aims relating to preparing children for something new came down heavily on the side of preserving the past. In this situation, evaluation of teaching methods and content was quite reasonably seen to be concerned with how well these outcomes were attained. The skills and knowledge were reasonably well defined and not too difficult to assess, and the curriculum was not constantly changing. However, in response to a society rapidly becoming more mobile, with a far greater variety of occupations becoming available, mass media, good transport and jobs which never existed before, education has become more concerned than before with preparation for the new. Instead of a son following in the footsteps and in the occupation of his father he has opportunities which were never open to his father. Whether he can grasp these opportunities, whether his ambitions are frustrated or achieved, depends not so much as before on his parents' status, but on his education. The questions asked about education, then, reflect the changing values of a significant section of society. Whilst it may well be that values held by the majority of the population have changed little, what is important is the greater change in the values of the minority, which includes most of those active in educational planning and renovation. It is among those who are able to influence education that there is greater value given to encouraging pupils to challenge and not accept, as previously, the assumptions and tenets of the past, to think for themselves, to query, to have confidence in their own powers of reasoning. There was no tradition of measuring these kinds of outcome, consequently the achievement strategy of evaluation was no longer capable of providing relevant information. Neither was there any certainty about how to bring about such outcomes, and so the information asked of evaluation was of the kind which would help decisions about developing the curriculum, not simply about whether or not it worked.

The power of schools and colleges to influence the prospects of their pupils is one of several recently growing pressures upon educational institutions and research workers to give account of what they do. When a curriculum innovation is introduced into a school, there are several interested bodies—LEAs, HM inspectors, school governors or managers, teachers' associations, parents

—who may want to know how it operates, what its effects are on pupils and teachers, why it is thought better than previous practice or alternative schemes. At the beginning of the 1960s, in the enthusiasm of the first wave of curriculum innovation, it was possible to say 'Look at how the children enjoy themselves when they are doing this work—of course it works.' It was true, too, because the change from previous learning experiences was so great. After a few more years and a few more waves of innovation, a far more precise description of the benefits from one innovation or another was required: more searching and sophisticated questions were being asked, and the enthusiasm for innovation *per se* had worn off.

One more factor influencing change in evaluation strategy should be mentioned here, though it is intended that this will be the subject of a full discussion in a later publication. A major theme in change in teaching methods has been towards catering for children as individuals rather than as a large group or class. The origins of this trend are complex, with roots in changes in society, in developments in educational psychology (led by Piaget and Bruner), and in the growing realization that traditional teaching methods take little account of motivation, attitudes or personal interest and fail to achieve affective aims. In rather different ways, Piaget and Inhelder (1969 and Bruner (1966) have said that children's ways of thinking should be taken into account in selecting learning experiences. Though they may have different views on how children learn, they agree that the optimum conditions for learning will vary for individual children and will depend on many factors, the chief of which are previous learning and experience, and stage of cognitive development. Their work has encouraged wider appreciation that to provide children with equal opportunities for learning means giving them different learning activities rather than equal learning experience—in other words, to adapt educational materials to the pupils rather than vice versa. The adaptation has to be either programmed into the materials or given into the hands of the teacher. In either case, the consequences for developing and evaluating curriculum materials which purport to cater for individual differences are profound. Evaluation must be concerned not only with the characteristics, variables and processes relating to the class as a whole, but also with individuals, each with his own set of abilities, preferences, styles of learning, attitudes, interests and past experiences. It is a formidable task to take account of all these factors and it requires a change in conception of what are relevant models for gathering and analysing the data.

MAJOR CHANGES IN QUANTITATIVE EVALUATION STRATEGY

The narrow view of evaluation as measurement of progress towards specified objectives originated in the application of a methodology more appropriate to experimentation in pure sciences than to the complex and imprecise process of curriculum development. Trials of new curriculum materials are regarded as tests of hypotheses that the use of the materials will result in certain specified changes in the pupils involved in the experiment. Not only does this approach assume that the intended changes can be measured, but it also implies that the 'treatment' is parcelled up in the materials and not appreciably influenced by the teacher, the pupils or other aspects of the learning environment. This approach is especially inappropriate for formative evaluation, where the point is not so much to find out whether or not the materials work as to gather information to improve both materials and their use. But it can also lead to inconclusive results in summative evaluation, notwithstanding experimental designs of considerable complexity, which are used in an attempt to control variables that might otherwise interfere with the experiment.

Some of the arguments concerned with experimental design illustrate the problems involved when an attempt is made to control the effect of influences apart from the curriculum material. In the first place, changes in pupil behaviours during the trial period cannot be assessed unless pre- and post-testing is carried out. But, in the second place, it is possible that concomitant experiences during the period may have been influential, or that the changes may have been the effect of maturation on the abilities and skills concerned. An obvious way to control such concomitant variables is to make comparisons, over the same period of time using the same measuring instruments, between changes in one group which is given the 'treatment' and another group which is not.

That this is not the simple solution it at first appears, however, is shown by the continuing arguments on the subject. Some of the problems of using controls arise from the inability to equalize all the variables; there is the intrusion of the 'Hawthorne effect' (Cook, 1962) when, as is generally the case, it is not possible to keep people unaware that they are an experimental group. Cronbach (1963) claims that it is impossible to eliminate the Hawthorne effect on the teachers in the way that doctors are able to neutralize the effect of awareness of treatment with experimental new drugs—by testing them in a 'double blind' design. Consequently, it can never be certain that any observed advantage of new curriculum materials is attributable to the materials themselves and not to the greater energy and application shown by teachers and students when trying things that are novel and have the prestige of being 'experimental'. Other problems come from the inability to produce tests which are fair to both experimental and control groups. When the performances of students studying an 'old' curriculum are compared with those of students studying a 'new' one, it is usually found that students on the new curriculum do better on test items designed for the new curriculum and worse on items designed for the old curriculum, whilst for students on the old curriculum the reverse is found (Scriven, 1967). Thus, it appears the results could be manipulated to favour either curriculum according to the relative balance of old-type and new-type items in the test.

To the first set of problems Scriven, an avid supporter of the use of control groups, proposes a solution which involves 'enthusiasm matching' (1967, p. 69). For this he suggests the production of various 'cut-rate new curricula' which are tried out by a series of control groups alongside the experimental group (p. 69). Since all groups are then trying something new, the enthusiasm should be the same for all. The ethics of this approach seem questionable, quite apart from the practicalities (Scriven cites no actual examples of its use), and though he may have made the point that in theory the problem is not insuperable, it seems doubtful whether his solution is a viable one. To the second set of problems, concerning the nature of the tests, Scriven also has an answer. He suggests that the items in a test should be weighted according to their merit as judged by subject-matter experts. As a result 'relatively minor improvements', in items relating to goals judged as important, are magnified and the effects of the new curriculum appear to be more favourable. Scriven goes on to make some cautionary remarks about this course of action, however, and expresses a major concern which must occur to most people hearing of this suggestion, that it is all too tempting to feel that the re-weighting must be correct because it supports the natural conviction of the innovators that the new curriculum must be better.

More elaborate and subtle research designs have been suggested, for example by Suchman (1967) and Brimer (1967), but frequently the result is no significant difference between trial and control classes. Despite Scriven's remark that 'no difference' is not 'no knowledge' (1967, p. 67), the lack of information provided by such a result forces reconsideration of whether this is the best way to evaluate curriculum materials. In fact, the information gain means little more, except in the satisfaction it brings, if significant differences are found. What is learnt then is that when most controllable variables are held constant, the material itself is effective in achieving objectives, but in practice the variables do influence the outcome and it is important to know more about the mechanism of this influence. For instance, it is likely that experiences prior to the trial period may affect the impact of experiences during the trial period. If differences between prior experiences are eliminated by choosing pupils with similar previous histories, then nothing can be learned about this variable. Many more faults of the strategy, which has been aptly labelled the 'agricultural–botany' model by Parlett and Hamilton, are detailed by them in Chapter 5 (pp. 85–8).

When put into practice, this classical experimental model, which seems logically attractive, fails to give the information which is most useful for either formative or summative evaluation. What makes it so attractive and reasonable is precisely its weakness: it is part of an over-simplified view of curriculum development as 'identification of objectives, planning of learning experiences, evaluation' (Wiseman and Pidgeon, 1970, p. 80), which ignores the characteristics of the learning environment and the interaction of learners and teachers with that environment, both in the development and in the evaluation stages. In reality, what pupils learn in any situation depends on a complex collection of factors, which have to be taken into account if the evaluation information is to be of practical value. There is no need to abandon measurement in order to produce a model of evaluation which is capable of encompassing more than the measurement of objectives. The strategy proposed by Wittrock (1970, p. 15) for example, shows the change towards a wider view of what evaluation should encompass:

A comprehensive approach to evaluating instruction would require us to make explicit and relate to each other the salient characteristics of: (i) individual learners, (ii) their instructional environments, and (iii) their learning, as these three exist in naturalistic settings. The concept of explicitness could then be extended to include learning, antecedent student behavior, and environmental characteristics of instruction. With the appropriate multivariate statistical tools for this approach we could estimate 'cause-and-effect relations' in the naturalistic data of evaluation studies.

Strategies taking into account more than measurement of goal achievement were discussed by Scriven (1967), in an article which pointed out the complexities of goals and roles of evaluation which should be clarified before a strategy suitable for any particular curriculum development is selected. He outlined the effects on the teachers, teachers' colleagues, other students not directly in contact with the materials, on administrators and parents, which may be significant and have a claim to be included in the scheme of evaluation. Although Scriven was critical in this paper of pure 'payoff' evaluation, he was nevertheless centrally concerned with outcomes rather than with the processes and conditions which lead to the outcomes. He attempted to develop a strategy which avoided some disadvantages of evaluation as assessment of goal achievement by proposing that information should be gathered about outcomes other than those expressed in the goals of the curriculum.

Recently he has developed this trend still further by espousing the notion of 'goal-free' evaluation. It seems from what he has written (1972) that he came to this idea through realizing that secondary effects or side-effects were often of crucial importance. The stated goals of projects, he says, are frequently couched in terms of 'in' phrases and high-sounding jargon; a proposal might sound good, but it was often more important to judge it with regard to its side-effects than to its goals as such. For the purpose of evaluation, then, any distinction between intended and unintended outcomes was irrelevant, and he arrived (1972, p. 1) at the surprising conclusion (surprising, that is, in the light of his earlier statements on the subject):

. . . that consideration and evaluation of goals was an unnecessary but also a possibly contaminating step. I began to work on an alternative approach—simply, the evaluation of *actual* effects against (typically) a profile of *demonstrated* needs in this region of education. I call this Goal-Free Evaluation.

Scriven provides a supporting argument based on an analogy between testing the effect of new drugs in medical research and testing the outcomes of a new educational programme. He suggests that when the investigator knows these should be something to look for, he searches more carefully than when a possible effect is unlikely to be found. ('After all, how can one seriously look for therapeutic results from a sugar-pill?'—1972, p. 3). Therefore the investigation should be 'blinded' as to what are the likely effects. It should be stressed that it is the *evaluation* which is goal-free in this strategy, not the curriculum planning. Scriven suggests that the curriculum development team should formulate its goals in testable terms but not disclose the goals to the evaluator, who should be looking for all outcomes, unbiased by whether they were intended or not.

To some extent Scriven rediscovered an approach to evaluation that Cronbach described very clearly several years previously. Cronbach, writing of formative evaluation, urged (1963, p. 683) that it should be concerned with description of outcomes 'in the broadest possible scale, even at the sacrifice of superficial fairness and precision'. Further, in his view, the evaluator's work is concerned with gathering any information which will help the curriculum developer make decisions leading to improvement in the materials. This is more a definition of evaluation than a strategy, but it leads to the kind of strategy described by Parlett and Hamilton in Chapter 5.

Thus, a line of development in empirical strategies can be traced, the changes to more widely based data gathering being brought about by dissatisfaction with results from information gained more 'scientifically' but more narrowly. Some examples from evaluations which illustrate different strategies are outlined below, following a look at the development of strategies which began as informal, impressionistic approaches to evaluation.

MAJOR CHANGES IN INFORMAL EVALUATION STRATEGY

It was suggested above that the model for evaluation adopted by some of the early curriculum development teams was derived from the work of inspectors. Inspectors look at a very wide range of processes, concomitants, conditions and outcomes of teaching and learning, but they do this subjectively and without in general quantifying their findings. The evaluation strategy which followed this approach thus gathered information widely, and in this respect seems to have begun where the discussion above of formal strategy ended up, but used methods which were intuitive and unreliable. A historical diversion into the origin and roles of HM inspectors is perhaps relevant, because it not only sheds light on the traditional faith in an inspector's professional, and yet personal, opinion, but also indicates the background to the suspicion and coolness which an evaluator sometimes encounters in schools.

The first HM inspectors were appointed in 1839 to inspect schools which received grants from public money. In the Minutes of the Committee of

Council of 1839 it was stated that 'the inspectors will not interfere with the religious instruction, or discipline, or management of the school, it being their object to collect facts and information, and to report the result of their inspections to the Committee of Council'. The Secretary for Education at the time, Dr James Kay-Shuttleworth, issued questionnaires to guide the work of inspectors, which he saw as encompassing the finances of the school, the sanitation and ventilation of the building, organization and discipline, teaching methods, adequacy of playgrounds, pupils' attendance, qualifications of teachers, and parent-teacher relationships. Interestingly, this list indicates a scope of activities which is still relevant to part of the inspectors' role today. As a result of the Revised Code in 1861, they became examiners of pupils, and indirectly the judges of teachers. Not surprisingly, teachers came to regard inspectors as their natural enemies and the legacy of poor relations between the two during the period of 'payment by results', which lasted until 1897, persisted well into this century. The suspicion of teachers about anyone who visits a school to collect information may well have originated in this experience and have been transmitted from one generation of teachers to the next.

At the beginning of this century, it was appreciated that inspectors should become more than reporters of whether a school was fulfilling the conditions for receiving public money (Ikin, 1944). Their work was to become constructive, aimed at improving teaching by bringing their experience to bear on all kinds of problems encountered by teachers. The dual aspects of an inspector's work are now seen as inspection and advice, with a growing emphasis on the latter (Central Advisory Council for Education (England), 1967). But assessing a school and its problems is a necessary precursor to giving advice, and an inspector is centrally concerned with forming a picture of the different circumstances, reasonable expectations and performance of different schools.

There are obvious similarities between part of the inspector's work and what is required for evaluating curriculum developments. To the pioneer projects of the early 1960s it seemed that here was a ready model and, in following it, members of project teams visited classes where the trial work was in action to observe as perceptively and objectively as possible. The job of gathering information was thought to require experience and the ability to judge, but not technical knowledge of assessment procedures or research methodology, so an 'evaluator' as such was not required. Unfortunately, it was inevitable that the team members who were writing the materials should suffer from what Scriven (1972, p. 2) describes as 'occupational tunnel-vision'—they generally saw what they wanted to see. The result was a collection of impressions, gained somewhat unsystematically, which could not be interpreted easily or generalized sufficiently for making decisions about the curriculum materials. Commenting on the evaluation of the early Nuffield projects, Kerr (1968, p. 15) points out that these decisions resulted 'from persuasive discourse in which each member of the team draws on his experience and personal judgment to arrive at a consensus of opinion'.

The informal approach generally gathers both empirical and non-empirical evidence. The empirical evidence comes from the trials, the classroom observations and reports from teachers, whilst the non-empirical evidence comes from opinion of experienced consultants who are asked to comment on the written materials. In both cases judgements are made quickly, often intuitively, and as a result of balancing a number of different factors against each other. However, judgement criteria are not made explicit and it is very difficult to say how valid or reliable such an assessment might be. In response to dissatisfaction with such uncertain information, strategies have been developed which use more objective procedures for gathering data from class-rooms and for studying the written materials.

In the case of classroom observations, certain procedures developed for analysing teaching behaviour provide an attractive means of collecting data objectively. Several techniques for interaction analysis have been produced, mainly for use in teacher education and in research on teacher effectiveness. The main features of this approach are explained in Chapter 4 (p. 72–3); at this point, the concern is with the implications of its use in terms of strategy. The results obtained from interaction systems can be used in two main ways: to follow the chain of events in a classroom and/or to find the frequency of events in each chosen category. The category system has, of course, to be designed to record the kinds of interaction relevant to an investigation. Thus N. A. Flanders's technique was originally devised for the purpose of assessing the proportion of teachers' 'direct' or 'indirect' teaching behaviour. To find this out, the frequencies in categories such as 'lecturing' and 'criticizing' were compared with frequencies indicating a less direct approach, such as 'questioning' and 'praising'. Some of the advantages of this strategy for curriculum evaluation are clear: it provides information, which can be readily quantified, about what actually happens when curriculum materials are being used (see, for example, Gallagher, 1970). A typical result is to show that materials which are intended to allow and encourage students to show initiative, to work through their own ideas, and so on, are teacher-dominated in practice. Moreover, the analysis produces a record of the kinds of dominant teacher behaviour involved, and this provides the information for revising the teachers' manuals or the preparation courses.

The strategy has disadvantages, however, from both a practical and a theoretical standpoint. On the practical side, the curriculum evaluator is likely to want to develop his own interaction system rather than use an existing one which may not quite suit his needs. Devising the schedules, obtaining and training observers, testing out the system, and making necessary changes before use, are extremely expensive and time-consuming activities, so an evaluator must consider carefully whether the results are likely to justify such a heavy consumption of resources. Whilst the new system will give an objective account of some classroom interactions, it inevitably gathers some useless information and misses opportunities (Stake, 1970). One of the theoretical disadvantages arises from the need to decide in advance precisely what are the elements to be observed: to analyse the variables so as to see possible classroom events as separate and discrete as well as in interaction with each other (Ober, Bentley and Miller, 1971). In consequence, if certain processes prove difficult to analyse or are not recognized as important, this may mean that they have to be left out of the observation frame, and in the same way unexpected processes and events may also be missed. Thus, interaction schedules are criticized for focusing only on those aspects of classroom behaviour which are easily classified but may be more trivial than subtler interactions, not readily isolated and defined but perhaps more important educationally. In passing, it is interesting to note a point made by Bealing (1973) that in correlation studies between teacher behaviours and pupil outcomes the most consistent findings have tended to emerge where high-inference rating scales were used, and not with low-inference measures. High-inference scales are far more readily devised than low-inference ones and, supported by other evidence, can be very useful, as illustrated by the instrument used in the evaluation of the Nuffield Secondary Science Project, which has been mentioned in Chapter 2 (p. 22) and is discussed at greater length in Chapter 6 (p. 120).

Turning now to the non-empirical evidence previously gathered by informal methods, there have been developments to make this also more systematic and more objective (see Chapter 4, p. 76). A technique developed for other purposes—content analysis—has been applied to the assessment of written materials by scrutiny. Widely used in many areas of research in literature and the social sciences, content analysis was not applied to educational evaluation until the late 1960s. Before this, judgements relating to style, emphasis and even content were non-systematic estimates, and the only guidelines given to the experts asked to give their opinions might be to 'comment upon how far the materials are child-centred, discovery-oriented, suitable for the age range, supportive of the general philosophy of the project', etc. When there is no attempt to define what is meant by 'discovery orientation' and how it would be recognized in the materials, then assessment of these qualities depends on the personal viewpoint of the expert. Only in the case of readability has there been widespread use of a systematic approach to analysis of written materials, but since a system developed for one type of subject-matter is not necessarily applicable to another, the results have not been wholly satisfactory (Grobman, 1972).

The object of content analysis is to 'measure' the content by classifying it in terms of defined criteria which could relate to many qualities—subject-matter, pedagogic methods suggested, underlying value systems, and so on.

In theory, any variable could be included which can be sufficiently well defined to meet the level of reliability which is thought acceptable. The profiles of curriculum materials thus obtained can be used in many ways. Perhaps the most obvious is to compare intention with reality: materials which purport to encourage creativity may have too many closed activities and not enough open-ended ones. The extent of coverage can be checked, the levels of cognitive demand estimated and compared with what might be reasonable to expect, or the final versions compared with trial versions to reveal the effect of rewriting materials.

The signs of danger in using this technique are present in its tendency to turn the analysis of materials into an automatic process, in which ticks are put on paper when certain features are identified. It follows the same tendency as interaction analysis, which could turn classroom observation into a matter of coding and recording. The result of the content analysis depends entirely on the schedule developed for it and can give no more information than the instrument is capable of recording. Thus the unintended will not be recorded and may not be noticed—and there remains the disquieting question, is the whole the sum of its parts? Less formal methods of non-empirical evaluation, though less objective, do not suffer from these particular disadvantages and provide useful information, particularly at the formative stage.

In summary, this discussion has shown that certain trends in techniques for examining content and processes have, in a curious way, made them more formal, and the strategies in which they are used are very similar to those which have evolved from the formal ones concerned with measuring achievement. The focus upon measurement of outcomes alone was found by many to be too narrow, and strategies have been suggested where this has been either superseded or heavily supplemented by other, less precisely gathered evidence. Meanwhile the opposite viewpoint, that evaluation was the job of on-the-spot experts, gave rise to dissatisfaction with subjective judgements and led to the development of strategies in which data of many different kinds could be gathered systematically with some measurable reliability. Ironically, it seems that the present trend is for the previously formal strategies now to become too informal, shedding less light in their attempt to be super-illuminative, and for previously informal strategies to become too narrow in gathering data, from over-concern to define criteria in behavioural or objectively identifiable terms.

SOME PRACTICAL EXAMPLES ILLUSTRATING CHANGING STRATEGIES

The following few examples of evaluation studies are chosen rather haphazardly from those which happen to be familiar to the author. They are no more representative or significant than others which might equally well have been cited and to which references are made throughout this book. The fact that the earliest example is also representative of an early point in the development of empirical strategies does not indicate that development of strategy is necessarily related to time; strategies far more narrow than the one Tyler used in the 1930s are still employed today. A trend with time may well be seen in the strategies used by individuals or teams, since evaluators learn from their own mistakes, but there seems a remarkable reluctance among evaluators to learn from the experience of others. What is written in weighty volumes by the acknowledged leaders in the field, mostly Americans, may seem attractive to the new evaluator, partly because it is neat and logical and uncluttered by untidy happenings of real life. Beside this, the views and experience of fellow evaluators not only lack the authority of the big names but appear to cloud the situation with 'ifs' and 'buts', the qualifying phrases which are often very relevant to the educational setting of work in this country. In fairness, however, it must be said that until the present time it has been difficult for evaluators to have access to accounts of work done in this country; the recent publication of the various reports referred to throughout this book and, hopefully, others to follow will do much to improve the opportunity for using earlier experience.

One of the landmarks in evaluation practice, and one which remained for perhaps two decades as the most thorough and well-documented account of a formative evaluation, is the Eight Year Study carried out under Tyler's direction in the 1930s (Smith and Tyler, 1942). Thirty high schools were taking part in the development of new learning programmes, and a special Committee on Evaluation and Recording was set up to develop means of appraising students' achievement and identifying the weaknesses of the programmes. The basic assumptions underlying the evaluation strategy were clearly stated and illustrate Tyler's view of evaluation. In the first place, it was assumed that education is a process which seeks to change the behaviour of students and the objectives of a programme should be expressed in terms of intended behaviour changes. Following on from this, it was assumed that appraisal of a school programme was the process of finding out how far the objectives are being achieved. Human behaviour was recognized as being extremely complex, requiring a battery of instruments to appraise its different aspects and relate these aspects to each other. Further, it was assumed that the instruments need not be limited to paper and pencil tests. The influence of evaluation on teaching was appreciated and seen as a challenge to develop techniques and instruments, which would be in line with the objectives of the new curricula and not restrictive. Finally, the evaluation was assumed to be the responsibility of the teachers, while the evaluation staff helped by developing instruments and methods of interpreting results. The intention, it was said, was to evaluate the programme and not the effectiveness of the school or the teachers.

Seven steps were outlined for the evaluation programme. The first three were concerned with formulating, classifying and defining objectives, leading to a list of statements expressed in terms of behaviours. The next three steps were concerned with devising batteries of test items. The final step involved working out ways of interpreting and using the results. One method was to compare earlier results with later results of the same students to assess progress; another was to work out norms against which to compare changes from year to year. Yet another was the study of inter-relationships between several scores in order to identify patterns of achievement. These methods enabled teachers to locate distortions in the patterns of development of their pupils, and thus suggest reasons for failure in particular areas or in particular pupils. The evaluation staff helped in devising methods of interpretation by discussing results with teachers, suggesting revisions in the programme, and indicating ways for investigating whether modifications had the desired effect.

From the point of view of evaluation strategy, the most important feature of this evaluation is that all the information fed back to modify the curricula came from the appraisal of students' behaviour changes, levels of achievement, or patterns of success. Apart from gathering base-line data about students' behaviours at the start of using the curriculum materials, the focus of the evaluation was upon what happened at the end. Attention was deliberately removed from the effect of the school environment or the teacher by the assumption that the evaluation was not concerned with these. When achievement was not found where it was expected, the instructional materials were assumed to be at fault and were modified. The changes were based on clues which could be picked up from the patterns of students' achievement and the hunches of the teachers and developers. The likelihood of false conclusions being drawn about the materials must be obvious to anyone who believes that the learning environment and the teacher's mediation can make all the difference between successful and unsuccessful use of materials. Further uncertainty about the validity of the feedback is added by considering the effect of specifying objectives in behavioural terms, especially in terms of testable behaviours. It is easy to find examples where the objectives were restricted to those behaviours which could be tested. Feedback was thus in terms of achievement within a narrowed range of outcomes. Not only were unintended outcomes left out of account but so also were intended ones which could not readily be expressed behaviourally and tested with acceptable objectivity.

Despite its shortcomings, this strategy did have advantages and remained a pattern which was advocated in texts on curriculum development and evaluation until well into the 1960s. It provided a neat picture of curriculum development in which evaluation had a well-defined function. It indicated how students' achievements could be used in modifying and developing materials. It provided for setting up criteria—the objectives—against which the value of curriculum materials could be assessed. It became, in fact, the 'classical' evaluation strategy.

It was little wonder, then, that an evaluator disposed to treat the gathering of data systematically and scientifically, rejecting the idea that personal judgement and opinion could be sufficient, would look in the first instance towards the classical strategy in searching for a model. The evaluator of the Oxford Primary Science Research Project (see p. 30) did just this. The result, however carefully analysed, could tell only about relative achievement of objectives; nothing was found out about possible reasons. In the case of these primary science materials, it became clear from the varying patterns of achievement from one class to another that reasons for the presence or absence of achievement were to be sought in the teachers' handling of the materials as much as in its content. The absence of information about the use of the materials and the management of learning activities stalled most attempts at interpreting the results.

It was possible to learn from this experience in planning the evaluation of the first draft materials of another and later science project, Science 5–13. The part played by the teachers' mediation between materials and pupils was expected to be considerable, so the formative evaluation programme included gathering information about classroom processes and interactions, about teachers' opinions and attitudes, as well as about children's achievement. During the development of the Science 5–13 materials, several sets of units were tried out at different times and the experience of earlier trials was used to improve the effectiveness of procedures and instruments for evaluating later trials. An outline of the major changes and the reasons for them will illustrate the kinds of shift in strategy which were described earlier in this chapter.

In the first set of trials the information collected was of four main kinds: about the achievement of objectives by the children, the learning environment, interactions in the classroom, and teachers' opinions and comments on the materials. The project's units were for teachers, who were expected to use the books as sources of activities to help children achieve objectives which were expressed in some detail and as far as possible in terms of behaviours. Much of the evaluation effort went into devising and administering tests to the pupils. The tests were designed to assess achievement of specific cognitive objectives of the units under test, more general cognitive objectives, and affective objectives of the materials. They were given as pre- and post-tests to approximately 2000 children taking part in the trials and an equal number of children acting as controls. During the trials, the classes were visited and information was recorded about the learning environment and the use being made of the materials by the teachers and children. The teachers completed three forms during the two-term trials, giving an account of their work, their opinions about the project in general and the unit they had tried in particular, and information about the background of their class and their own experience.

Detailed analysis of test results showed where there had been differences between trial and control groups on items relating to particular objectives, but in few cases were the differences of statistical significance (at the 0·05 level). One reason for this must have been the low reliability of the tests, arising partly from the small number of items for each objective (kept small to minimize interference with the trial work) and partly because, in formative evaluation, there is not time to refine tests sufficiently before they are used. But a more important reason was that change in score was very much influenced by other factors than the trial work. For example, it was found that change in score among the trial classes was inversely and not directly related to a measure of the teacher's grasp of the project's philosophy and satisfactory use of the unit. A quite reasonable explanation for this was eventually suggested by further examination of the results. Large increases in a class's mean scores were more likely when pre-test scores were low rather than high, and low initial scores were associated with the children's previous experience being of formal teaching with little opportunity for first-hand activity and problem-solving. The effect of working actively during the trial work, even though their learning experiences may not have been as satisfactory as would have been wished, enabled them to perform at a considerably higher level in the post-test; hence the large increase in their scores. Conversely, children used to exploring at first hand were able to perform well on the pre-test and showed a smaller improvement, even though their activities during the trial period may have been very satisfactory. Of course, pre-test score levels were affected by many other factors as well as previous experience in school, and it was impossible to separate and control this variable. It was clear, then, that many factors confounded the interpretation of children's test scores, which meant that they could not be taken as measurements of the effect of the trial work. Relative achievement of different objectives was the most useful information derived, but its low reliability meant that it had to be supported by information from other sources. The question has to be asked: would the test results have been more helpful had they been more sensitive? There would then have been more certainty about whether there had been progress towards achievement of particular objectives, but this would not have reduced the uncertainty as to the causes of change or lack of it.

In further analysis of the evaluation data, the information for each class about changes in mean scores were put together with all other items from the visitor's report, and the codable responses from the teachers' questionnaires. A computer programme for classifying qualitative data (Brimer, 1968)—a form of cluster analysis—was used. Groups of items were identified, representing the strongest dimensions, or themes, in the patterns to be found in the data. From these it was possible to find the conditions and circumstances of using a unit which had been associated with different opinions and comments upon it. With the help of this analysis, the varied reactions of teachers to the materials could be interpreted in terms of the background of use from which they arose. It was possible to suggest reasons for dissatisfaction and to use this information in revising the draft materials. More details about this evaluation can be found elsewhere (Harlen, 1975), but the main points of relevance to emerge from it were that the information useful for the formative evaluation came not from the results of testing children but from gathering information by observation in the classroom to provide a basis for interpreting opinion, comments and other outcomes.

In trials of later sets of the project's units, more of the evaluation effort was put into gathering evidence about processes in the classroom and about the effect of the work on the teachers. Assessment of progress among the children was made by the teacher using a method designed essentially to help her identify behaviours related to the objectives. Children were also interviewed by the classroom observer, the results contributing valuably to a picture of the interactions between teachers, pupils and materials. The data gathered, and their analysis using the programme mentioned above, enabled the evaluation to fulfil its role of providing information which would guide revision of the units to make them more helpful to more teachers. It seemed that this role was best served by regarding the goal of the evaluation as being to examine the processes in operation during the use of the materials, rather than to assess achievement of objectives. This was not to deny that a curriculum has ultimately to be validated by its effect upon pupils; but in short-term trials changes in pupils' behaviours can be too much influenced by factors other than the trial work to be of much use in formative evaluation. The change in strategy, from focusing on outcomes to focusing on processes, was brought about by the practical problem of trying to make sense out of the complexities of a real situation. It was borne on the evaluator that it is necessary to look at the effect of trial work in a far broader way than was initially supposed. The system of which the class and teacher are only parts is complicated indeed, and the introduction of new ideas and materials into it can be affected by, and have repercussions for, aspects which are not easy to anticipate.

Conclusions of a similar kind were reached independently by others working in different fields of curriculum evaluation. The work of Parlett at Massachusetts Institute of Technology provides an illustration of the 'illuminative' approach, the strategy designed to discover rather than assume the aspects of the system which might be relevant to curriculum change. The innovation being evaluated was the introduction of the method of 'concentrated' study in a higher education science course (Parlett and King, 1971). Instead of the usual practice of spreading the course, in this case Physics III, over many months and alongside several other subjects, in concentrated study the course was completed in four weeks and no other subjects were studied during that time. The length of the course was not the only new feature, however; there were innovations in teaching methods, experiences and opportunities for students. For instance, in the normal course there was no laboratory work, and the students were taught through formal lectures, seminars in large groups and weekly assignments. In the concentrated study course, laboratory work was a central feature and there was emphasis on informality and small group work. Evidently there were many differences between the normal and the experimental course, and no attempt was made to set up an evaluation which would compare the two. Neither were the aims of the course stated in terms of students' behaviours; instead, they were expressed in terms of processes and interactions during the course, for example (1971, p. 2): 'to enable the teacher to work with students in a less impersonal context than is afforded by lecturing; to stimulate informed discussion . . . to introduce a far wider range of activities . . .'

As there were only twenty students taking part in the experimental class, the investigator was able to gather at first hand all the information he wanted. Information was gathered in three ways: by observation during classes, through interviews with students and discussions with the instructor and his assistants, and from questionnaires given to the students.

Information is thus derived from several different sources. This permits a more comprehensive investigation that would be possible utilizing few different techniques. It also enables particular questions and issues related to COS [concentrated study] to be approached from different angles, with systematic cross-checking and comparison of information derived from several sources. [1971, p. 10]

With so many different kinds of data to relate to each other, it is clearly difficult to be exhaustive in searching for themes and patterns within it. Patterns can be sought comprehensively in qualitative data, as in the case of Science 5–13, but in this instance there was no such analysis. Instead, Parlett chose to pose certain questions relating to the conditions and effects of the experimental course and to present, frequently in anecdotal form, the evidence from various sources which helped to answer these questions. Examples of the questions are: 'How hard did they [the students] work?' 'What were the chief differences between concentrated study and the normal method of distributed study, from the student's point of view?' 'How did the students get on together?' 'Did they learn as much?' In answer to the last question, evidence came from students' opinions of how well they thought they had learned the subject-matter. There were no examinations at the end of the course, and no tests were given for the purpose of evaluating students' achievement. The reason is probably to be found in Parlett's comment (1971, 23n): 'The assumption that exam results serve as an adequate criterion of competence, understanding and retention is, anyway, extremely dubious. It presupposes—instead of questioning—their legitimacy and relevance for such purposes.' It might also be added that in this situation, where so many and various changes may have influenced different students to different degrees, the interpretation of short-term changes in behaviours would have been so difficult that the results might well have been almost valueless.

As a result of this illuminative evaluation, the investigator was able to conclude (1971, p. 27) 'that the experiment on the whole was successful, our hopes and hypotheses being largely fulfilled'. It was also possible to detail the ways in which the students had benefited more from this course than from previous normal physics courses, and to list advantages for the instructor. There was a marked lack of critical comment about the experiment—which may have been because the new course was so good and the old one so dreadful, in this case, or because there was a marked Hawthorne effect (see above, p. 34) which gave this impression—but it may also be inherent in the evaluation strategy. When the evaluator puts himself so much inside the materials or method being tried, there must be empathy between him and those taking part in the experiment, and his attitude has to be positive or he would be in danger of undermining the confidence of the participants. Then judgement may become less objective than is desirable.

SOME MAJOR ISSUES WHICH AFFECT CHOICE OF STRATEGY

Three of the major issues which confront an evaluator when he is making decisions about the overall framework of his work are chosen for discussion here. The first can be called the 'scale or scope' issue: whether to gather data from a large sample but accept the restricted variety of instruments which can be used in large-scale operations, or whether to gather a wider range of different kinds of data from a smaller sample. The next concerns the attention to be given to the goals of the curriculum innovation: going beyond the question of whether to test achievement of objectives, the problems confronted here are whether the study should encompass unintended as well as intended outcomes, or whether it should attempt to monitor all outcomes without foreknowledge of which ones were intended. Thirdly, there is the issue of the relative emphasis on process or product: whether the evaluation should be more concerned to look at the transactions whilst the materials are being used, or more directed towards investigating end-products, the objectives of the curriculum. In all these issues there are few generally applicable guidelines to follow; each evaluator has to resolve the issues after considering the purpose and setting of his investigation and, particularly, the use to be made of the information he gathers. The pros and cons must be weighed carefully, since the decisions made by the evaluator in these matters influence the nature of the data he gathers and the information he can provide.

The line of strategies whose roots were in experimental psychology employ large samples in the interests of randomizing uncontrolled variables and producing generalizable results. The criticism made by Hamilton and Delamont of this approach as it refers to interaction analysis research (1974, p. 3) is equally true of other kinds of information treated in this way:

Such an approach (even if it can achieve true randomness) may fail to treat local perturbations or unusual effects as significant. Indeed, despite their potential significance for the classroom or classrooms to which they apply, atypical results are seldom studied in detail. They are treated as 'noise', ironed out as 'blurred averages' and lost to discussion.

What seems to be emerging is a change from extensive large sample inquiries to intensive small sample ones. Many features of large samples which are regarded as virtues in experimental research are no longer advantages if they lead to differences between classes, or between pupils, being ignored rather than investigated. Nevertheless, the dangers inherent in using small samples cannot be ignored.

Frequently cost, in terms of manpower, time and financial expense, is the most important factor which forces an evaluator to consider the relative advantages of scale and scope. Without cost restrictions, most would probably go for both scale and scope. Basically the problem is that if it seems desirable to collect a number of different kinds of information about each pupil, teacher, group or class, then there is a limit to the size of population which could be included. In practice it may mean, for example, that time available for 100 visits can be used to visit 50 classes twice or 10 classes five times each. The decision may be that the former is preferable if the value of the information would be increased more by having sampled a range of circumstances and approaches than by more frequent visiting. Such may be the case where classroom transactions are of a similar kind throughout a course. Alternatively, where it may be misleading to generalize observations from a small number of visits, the balance might be in favour of a more intense study of fewer classes or individuals. Thus, the choice must be made within the particular context of the evaluation concerned. Few evaluators will have sufficient resources to ignore this issue, though perhaps more could adopt the kind of compromise devised and used by MacDonald (1973, p. 89) in the evaluation of the Humanities Curriculum Project already referred to in Chapter 2 (p. 20):

The work contains clinical, psychometric and sociometric elements. Basically, information has been sought from two overlapping school samples, one large and one small, the idea being to study in some detail over a period of time the experience of a small number of schools, while gathering sufficient information about what was happening in a large number of schools to permit interpretation from one sample to the other.

At another level than the practical, a decision about the issue of scale and scope reflects a certain viewpoint about the purpose of evaluation in a particular development. On the one hand, scale is important where measurement is regarded as central to the role of evaluation. Differences or changes which are not statistically significant with a small sample may well become so with a larger sample, though the change for any individual pupil or class is no greater and no more significant as a result. On the other hand, where the purpose of evaluation is regarded as explanatory, to find out and describe different effects and conditions associated with successful adoption of an innovation, then scope is vastly more important. The point is well made by Stake, when he writes (1967b, p. 5) that a full evaluation 'tells what happened. It reveals perceptions and judgements that different groups and individuals hold . . . It tells of merit and short-coming. As a bonus, it may offer generalization . . .'

The second issue has recently been crystallized as the goal-based versus goal-free evaluation argument. Like the scale or scope issue, the way it is resolved in any particular instance will be influenced by the evaluator's general conception of his work and by the value judgements he is prepared to make. It is easy to dismiss so-called goal-free evaluation by saying that it is not logically possible for the process to ever be goal-free; it can be free from the confines of the goals of the programme being evaluated, perhaps, but not free of the goals of the innovation in a wider context (Alkin, 1972). However, to dismiss the notion without at least considering the reasons which gave rise to it would be to ignore some major questions. The ideal strategy of goal-free evaluation has two important advantages over goal-based evaluation. First, it gathers information about all effects which seem to the evaluator to be worthy of attention and, secondly, it gathers information and determines the relative importance of various effects without the bias likely to be introduced by knowledge of what were intended and unintended effects. Scriven, as noted above (p. 38), goes so far as to say (1972) that the evaluator should not read the objectives of the curriculum materials or discuss intended outcomes with the developers. But the arguments he uses indicate a view which regards an educational innovation as a 'treatment' and evaluation as measurement of a variety of results, both expected and unexpected, from using it. Within this view, anything which widens the scope of the information collected is to be welcomed. The ideas behind the goal-free strategy take much of the narrowness from the 'measurement of achievement' approach, but the emphasis remains on product assessment.

When evaluation is regarded as having a wider purpose, such as is indicated by Stake in the words quoted above, there is in any case much less emphasis on goal measurement and already a search for changes in many different aspects of the system into which change is introduced. An evaluation which looks at all likely effects and circumstances, in order to inform those who have to make decisions about the innovation, is in some respects of its nature goal-free. Yet the evaluator working in this way would not necessarily think it a virtue to be innocent about the goals of the materials.

There are many reasons why he should want to know the goals, and in any case it would be very difficult in practice not to know them. The issue then is whether the evaluator can be as objective in selecting the information to be gathered if he knows the intended goals as when he does not. The danger which is suggested is that, in choosing the emphases of his evaluation programme, he will tend to put more effort into areas of expected consequences and may miss important unexpected ones. There seems little an evaluator can do to avoid the problem other than be aware of it and consciously minimize the tendency to be influenced by knowledge of the goals. Evaluators are, after all, human, and this is not the only source of bias to which they may be subject. The very fact that the goal-free or goal-based issue has been raised and widely discussed is a measure of how far strategies have changed; not so long ago the job of clarifying objectives was defined as an essential component of evaluation (Taba, 1962).

The third issue which has to be faced in deciding an evaluation strategy concerns processes and products. Generally, information about both of these is desirable, but there are occasions when the evaluation must effectively concern itself with processes only. The timing of the evaluation and its role in the curriculum development have a strong influence in deciding this issue. If products are measured when not only are the materials in draft form but teachers and pupils are also unfamiliar with them and either struggling to adapt themselves or adapting the materials to their traditional way, then the question arises as to what exactly the results measure. It is necessary for the independent variables to be in operation before it is worth while measuring the dependent variable (Glaser, 1970); therefore in a formative evaluation the emphasis is most usefully placed upon the processes taking place. Even when processes are nearer to those envisaged by the developers, the results from testing outcomes during formative evaluation are very likely to be influenced by variables which may have a greater effect in the short term than the new materials. Indeed, there may be danger in assessing outcomes too soon, for any change in a positive and expected direction may be taken as evidence that the processes were in operation and were effective, when this might not be the case at all.

There is, however, an equal danger in focusing only on processes if the assumptions that they lead to desired products are never actually tested. It may be legitimate, as well as practical, to concentrate upon the way the materials are operating and on improving this before testing for outcomes in the pupils—except that so often the necessary follow-up never takes place. Even if it does take place, it seems fair to ask what will happen if at that stage negative results are obtained, that is, if the summative evaluation reveals that the assumptions on which both the materials and the formative evaluation strategy were based are invalid. It is tempting to say that products should be tested from the start in order to guard against this possibility, but negative results at earlier stages could most likely be explained in terms of uncontrolled variables and the inadequacy of early draft materials. Formative trials of the usual kind are no place to test basic hypotheses about consequences of classroom procedures and learning situations; the dilemma remains.

A solution to the problem may be to have two kinds of evaluation going on in parallel during the formative stage of the curriculum project. One of these would test the assumption that the various learning activities and methods embodied in the materials do lead to the achievements and changes which are claimed for them. It would be a comprehensive investigation on a small scale, but carried out over a period of two or more years. Only a few classes would be required, but these would be carefully chosen and prepared so that the processes and conditions of learning as envisaged by the developers were in operation as near to their ideal as possible. No effort should be spared to help the teachers put the developers' ideas into practice, for this is the proving ground of the approach. The products of the process would be monitored over an extended period of years, so that middle-term as well as short-term effects could be observed. Of course the long-term outcomes and those not easily defined would no more be known by this approach than any other, but the results would at least allay doubts about some of the outcomes.

Alongside this empirical test of ideas, the second type of evaluation would be proceeding. This would provide information about attempts to put the intended processes into action on a larger scale. Outcomes need not be monitored, so the evaluation could concentrate upon the events in and around the classroom and the general setting of the innovation. Setting up these large-scale trials and devising material for them frequently takes about two years and often requires pilot trials in a small number of classes. By this time, some results from the empirical test of outcomes would be available, either to suggest that the procedures envisaged were satisfactory or to indicate modifications which might be made. The large-scale trials would provide data for decisions about the feasibility of the ideas in normal situations, and the kinds of help or preparation which might be given to teachers, heads or even administrators wishing to implement the innovation.

The separation of process and product evaluation in this way has the advantage that each is investigated without the confusion of uncertainty in the other. The products are assessed in conditions where the processes are known to be in operation as intended; the processes are observed without the intrusion of doubt as to whether or not they are worth while in terms of outcomes. The two might fit into an evaluation programme along the lines suggested in Fig. 2. In some instances, where a curriculum development project is spreading ideas which are already in operation in a few places, the selection of the sample for the empirical test of ideas could be from good examples of these classes or schools. Where there is a greater degree of innovation, not only would the setting up of classes exemplifying good

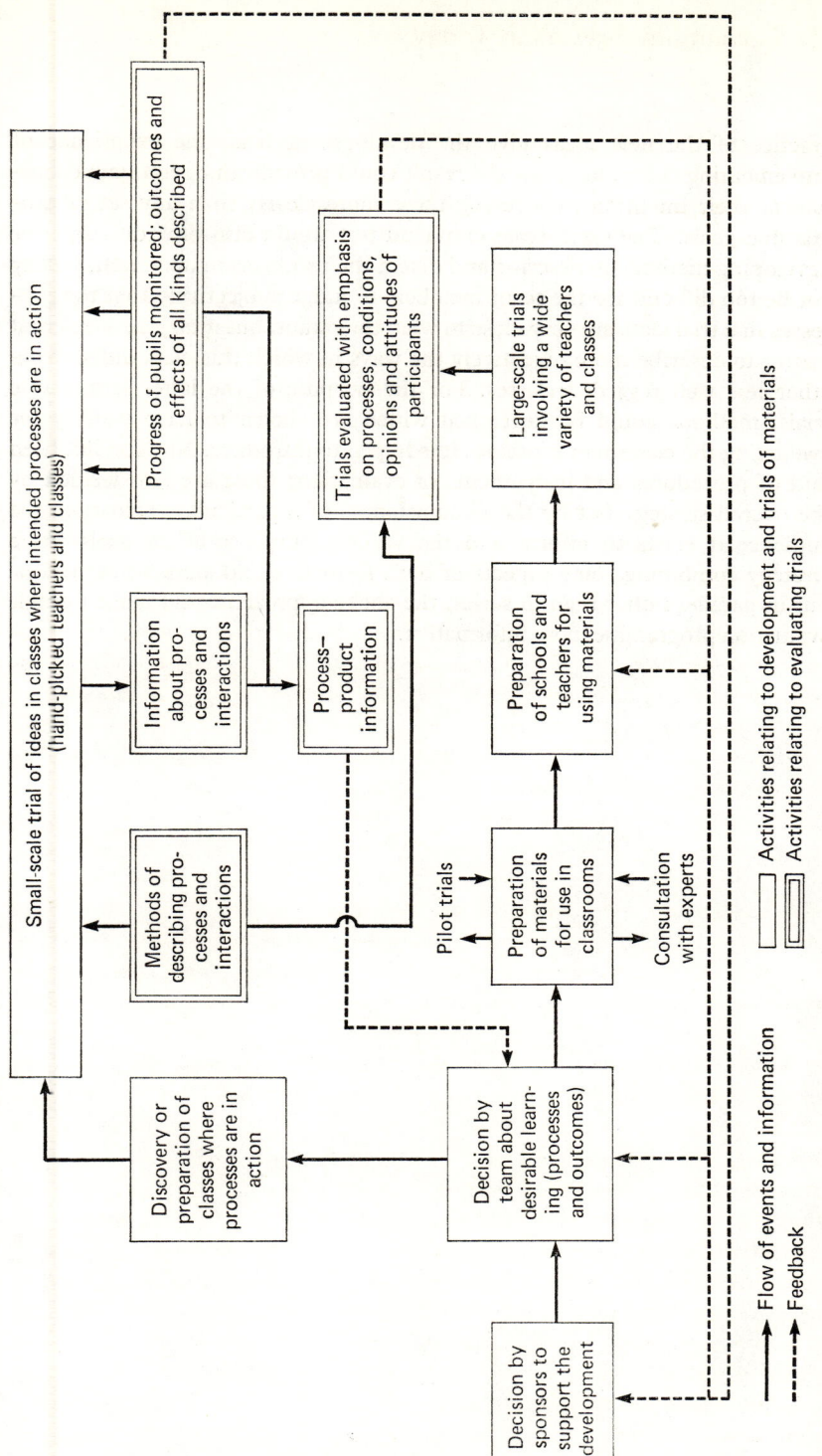

Fig. 2 A strategy for approaching the process-product issue in evaluation

Small-scale trial of ideas in classes where intended processes are in action (hand-picked teachers and classes)

Progress of pupils monitored; outcomes and effects of all kinds described

Information about processes and interactions

Process–product information

Methods of describing processes and interactions

Trials evaluated with emphasis on processes, conditions, opinions and attitudes of participants

Large-scale trials involving a wide variety of teachers and classes

Preparation of schools and teachers for using materials

Pilot trials

Preparation of materials for use in classrooms

Consultation with experts

Discovery or preparation of classes where processes are in action

Decision by team about desirable learning (processes and outcomes)

Decision by sponsors to support the development

⎯→ Flow of events and information

------→ Feedback

▭ Activities relating to development and trials of materials

▤ Activities relating to evaluating trials

practice of the new ideas give the development team the experience of implementing their ideas, but the result could provide an operational definition of their intentions, conveying these more clearly than any set of programme goals. The small-scale empirical test would also provide scope for developing methods to describe and detect the processes in operation. It may not be too difficult for the team members to judge subjectively that the processes in a trial class are very close to what they want, but it may be a different matter to describe more objectively the ways in which this class differs from other less well regarded classes. For the purpose of the latter larger-scale trials, methods could be developed which are shown to have validity for evaluating the classroom processes it is hoped to introduce. Nothing has been said of procedures and instruments of evaluation: these are not decided by the overall strategy but by the circumstances of a particular evaluation, the audience it exists to inform and the various purposes of its trials. As a strategy combining some aspects of both formative and summative studies, but in parallel rather than in series, the above approach could make a single evaluation programme more informative.

4 Techniques of evaluation

Stephen Steadman

This chapter aims to serve three groups of readers: those seeking to
know what techniques are used in evaluation; those who wish to know
enough about the techniques to judge the information offered in an
evaluation report; and potential evaluators wanting to know what
techniques are available. The techniques may be grouped according
to whether they provide formative feedback, test levels of attainment,
measure changes in attitude and motivation, or attempt to describe the
curriculum processes involved. The constraints which apply to the
application of these techniques in the conditions of active curriculum
development have to be appreciated, if reliance upon the information
they supply is not to be misplaced.

PRELIMINARY CONSIDERATIONS

In the other chapters of this book it is made abundantly clear that there is no
single all-purpose model of an evaluation. Harlen (Chapter 3) has described
the changes of approach which have produced what may now be thought of as
a continuum of available models. The range is from the classical attempts to
measure the achievement of objectives, to models which stress description of
the context and the quality of interactive effects—intended or otherwise.
Chapter 5 sees Parlett and Hamilton proposing an illuminative model of
evaluation which involves approaches and methods at the latter end of this
continuum and, incidentally, saying hard things of the opposite end. All this
apparent orderliness is very reassuring. There is a non-monopolistic situation—critical arguments designed to test the appropriateness of different
models flourish—and one might almost be tempted to think in terms of
'best buys'. But, in a very real sense, this orderliness is only apparent. It may
well be that to talk in terms of 'models' is a *post hoc* exercise which lends
respectability to the eclectic approaches adopted in practice. For it often
happens that evaluation is an afterthought, carried out by evaluators short of
time and resources.

To anyone who tries to understand the information offered by evaluators, it is often more germane to consider the appropriateness of the exercise on a different level. Such a person might pose three questions:

(a) What are the special features of this evaluation (or curriculum development) which are of interest to me?
(b) What are the appropriate techniques to investigate these aspects of the situation?
(c) Which techniques were in fact used?

The answers to these questions will often do more than merely satisfy the inquirer as to the validity of the evaluation from his point of view. For, in situations where he has expected certain techniques to be applied yet they have not been, the explanation of the discrepancy (if not incompetence!) is likely to offer new insights.

What follows in this chapter is an attempt to provide a framework for understanding evaluation reports at this level of contrasting the available techniques with those techniques actually chosen and applied. Hopefully, three groups of readers will be served: those who wish to know what substance lies behind the title of evaluation; those who wish to judge the information offered in an evaluation report; and potential evaluators who may wish to select appropriate techniques for use. The aim has been to provide brief details and supplement these with examples from actual projects and references to the literature as appropriate. The examples drawn from project experiences come in the main, but not without exception, from Schools Council projects—past and present.

DEFINITION AND DESIRABLE PROPERTIES OF TECHNIQUES

When does a technique become a methodology, a methodology a style? When does a style qualify for the title of a model? Considerations of this sort are not as important as they first appear, and closely argued definitions are not required. The position adopted in this exposition has been to conceive of the following hierarchy: techniques and methods, methodologies and styles, models—in ascending order of generality of compass. However, these distinctions have not been pursued rigorously. 'Techniques' and 'methods' are used interchangeably and, when wider descriptions have become necessary, 'methodologies' or 'styles' are referred to.

This approach to the problem of definition means that the techniques and methods of evaluation might be described as comprising those activities that an evaluator engages in to obtain and analyse his data. Such a description leaves aside the question of determining which aspects of an innovation require the evaluator's attention and the associated decisions on which techniques to employ. These matters are settled at the level of an evaluator's choice of methodology and style of working—dealt with in other chapters. The techniques which are available to evaluators may be described in terms largely independent of such decisions.

Settling the issue of definition in this way brings us to examine the desirable properties of evaluative techniques. From one point of view evaluation provides evidence for decision-makers and, in so far as this is true, a corollary of this purpose would be that an evaluative technique should provide information which is valid, reliable, germane to the concerns of the decision-maker, and available in time to inform the decisions. These are very generalized properties. In the following pages the properties of techniques are considered in relation to the purposes they may serve in an evaluation programme. To this end, the techniques have been considered in relation to the four major areas which inevitably receive the attention of present-day evaluators: the provision of formative feedback; the measurement of attainment; the assessment of attitude, interest and motivation; and the description of the curriculum context and processes. This is an intentionally broad schema, with obvious overlapping in that the latter three areas may all provide data for formative feedback. However, it reflects the current concerns of evaluators and has an additional advantage in blurring the distinction between 'objective' and 'subjective' techniques—a distinction often made but now outwearing its usefulness. Most important, if techniques are examined in relation to these four areas of concern to evaluators, then anyone wishing to answer the three questions raised at the start of this chapter has a clear indication of where to look for the answers. (For an alternative description of techniques see Grobman, 1968.)

FORMATIVE FEEDBACK TECHNIQUES

All evaluation supplies feedback in some sense or other. But the meaning here is confined to finding out how the ideas and materials of a project are received during the period of their development. Essentially, the information supplied guides decisions on what changes should be made and this implies some necessary and sufficient conditions if the evidence gathered is to be convincing enough to make the project team question its own work. It is absolutely necessary that the feedback be supplied in time for the information to be incorporated into revised approaches, and the evidence produced must also be psychologically sufficient if changes are to result. Especially is this so when it is the project's ideas which are under criticism. While projects are psychologically prepared to make changes in 'draft' materials or their tentative recommendations about teaching approaches, it is rare to find instances of a development team changing its fundamental rationale or basic premises in response to feedback from teachers, pupils or anyone else. If the intrinsic aims of the development are to be challenged, it is only to be done by the judgement of a peer group. Teachers judge teachers. Curriculum developers judge curriculum developers.

By looking at the requirements of a credible feedback in this fashion, the limitations of feedback from teachers and pupils to a central team may be envisaged. Changes are only likely to be made on the basis of teacher or pupil reactions when those reactions and opinions are seen to be based upon specialist experience. Obviously, classroom practice is such experience, but it is no use obtaining teacher opinion unless it is on a topic upon which the recipients are willing to allow that the teacher is a qualified expert. Otherwise, the information will be held to point to the need to change the teacher's opinions, not the need for changes in the project or its output.

In a decentralized system, the crucial factor in deciding between success and failure of a curriculum development project is the opinion teachers come to hold of its aims and activities. Therefore feedback to the developers, giving details of teacher opinion, is vital if there is to be any interaction. The methods used to provide such feedback are simple and direct. Projects have commonly employed *questionnaires, checklists, teacher diaries, group discussions* and formally convened *evaluation conferences*, which offer teachers the time and stimulation to elaborate their criticisms; but the mainstay of all feedback is the *personal interview*.

Questionnaires and checklists
It is when a project is producing teaching materials that these instruments are most often employed. From the examples of feedback questionnaires shown in the Appendix as Forms A–E it may be seen that, whatever the differences in layout, there are underlying similarities. Because it is the usual intention to supplement the questionnaire responses by interviewing at least some teachers, many of the questions are heavily structured—rating and ranking scales being freely used. This use of precoded response patterns helps an evaluator to collate replies, an essential matter when dealing with many schools, but it places heavy responsibilities upon him. Key questions arise from three sources: the writers of the materials will have in mind certain issues requiring clarification; previous interviewing will have spotlighted facets that teachers seem worried about; the evaluator too will have additional questions which might relate to issues raised by other interested parties such as LEA advisers, or anticipate requirements of the project at a later stage.

The writer's queries are usually centred upon the effectiveness of the materials; estimates of the time it takes to cover a unit of work; whether the level of language is appropriate to the age group being taught and other similar matters closely tied to the teaching materials. Teachers are likely to share the concern about these aspects but, in addition, may want to indicate problems of classroom and child/pupil management. For example, when the Nuffield (O level) Physics courses were being introduced into schools, problems of equipment storage and retrieval had to be reckoned with.

Posing questions on these levels produces instruments which look crude and unsophisticated and which yet hide a delicate balancing of interests. There is seldom time to refine a questionnaire between successive writing cycles except in the most elementary of fashions, and sometimes different questions must be asked in successive questionnaires. Most projects have time for only one trial of materials in a large number of schools before a final revision is made for the publishers and, in special circumstances, this is just not sufficient to provide for adequate revision of materials. The Continuing Mathematics Project is developing programmed learning materials for sixth formers. There is a three-stage revision cycle; pilot or developmental testing in a very small number of schools local to the project's headquarters, field testing in 10–15 schools, validation testing in 30 or so schools and other institutions. Feedback is obtained by questioning students in the pilot testing and by questionnaire in the last two cycles (see Appendix).

Ideally, the construction of opinion questionnaires and checklists should be undertaken with the same kind of stringency that is expected in the construction of attitude scales and attainment tests. The realities of the time scale make this impossible in the context of curriculum development inspired by short-lived projects, so what should be done to minimize the inevitable shortcomings of the use of checklists or questionnaires? A brief answer might be to observe the following guides:

(*a*) Be sure that the questions you ask are ones that the teacher can answer.
(*b*) Observe the same kind of rules which govern the construction of an attitude scale; e.g. at its most simple, don't use four grades A–D for the expression of approval. Everyone will answer B.
(*c*) Consider carefully the sample of teachers from whom you draw opinion.
(*d*) Arrange to cross-check opinions against the opinions of others, e.g. teachers' with pupils'.
(*e*) Use more than one method of collecting information.

For guidance in design and use see Moser (1967) and Oppenheim (1966).

Teacher diaries
These feature in many programmes of formative evaluation, because it is important to know how much time has actually been spent on the project, especially in primary schools. At their simplest, they provide spaces for pupils' progress to be monitored in terms of how many work units have been completed (see Form F in the Appendix). Usually there is also space for comments on difficulties experienced with equipment, preparation time, etc. If teachers can be persuaded to complete them regularly, and not in a rush immediately prior to an evaluator's visit, they offer a quick indication of slowing down in the work, which alerts an evaluator to possible loss of pupil or teacher motivation, errors in the level of difficulty of materials, and other causes for concern. Diaries also offer a gauge of the involvement of a teacher

in the project, and clues as to the teacher's degree of objectivity about his own methods. The drawbacks to their use can lie in the sporadic way in which some are completed and in the heavy demands they can make on a teacher's time. Frequently they are the most resented parts of a project's presence in a school.

Instead of supplying a separate work progress sheet and diary, some projects have encouraged teachers to make jottings in the margin of trial texts, recording little more than the date and their reactions as the work progresses. It is important for an evaluator to know about these spontaneous reactions which new forms of working evoke, and the teacher's rough notes of praise or condemnation, of pupil comments, or of difficulty with equipment, provide a contemporary record which is easily amplified in discussions between the teacher and evaluator. This form of record-keeping appears natural to most teachers and supplies much of the information a more formal diary would provide.

Group discussions and evaluation conferences
When a more general feedback is necessary and a fuller exposition of attitudes, opinions and doubts is desired, the convening of an evaluation conference is often the answer, particularly when the project is concerned to alter teaching methods. The possible gains are real and of a separate kind from those obtained from either questionnaires or personal interviewing.

At a group discussion, teachers are provided with the group identity that is often needed before they are willing to offer seriously critical comments, whereas the interview, when one teacher faces one evaluator, is obviously open to the influence and bias that any one-to-one discussion allows. The teacher's readiness to state his opinions is moderated by his perception of the evaluator's role but, in a group, the teacher's consciousness of this role may be lessened. A second advantage is that the teachers, in talking with one another, take account of the differing experiences of their colleagues and unconsciously modify their criticisms. Not that they cease to offer genuine opinion; rather, they tend to disregard those critical opinions of their own that they now see to be peculiar to their own special circumstances. Extreme pressures for change on the basis of individual experiences are therefore toned down without the intervention of a team member.

It must be recognized that a few teachers sometimes seem to seek to justify their expertise to colleagues by adopting extremely critical attitudes to the project or some aspects of its work. This can unnecessarily restrict the scope of discussion in a group if the structure is left too loose and, at conferences, it can lead to the formation of pressure groups with similar results. Individuals known to have this tendency can be given the position of explaining a part of the project's work, which enables them to demonstrate their expertise less destructively. It may also be useful to draw sharp distinctions between sessions designed to evoke all shades of criticism and constructive sessions at which the repetition of purely negative stances is discouraged.

However, any conference must be carefully planned and recorded. At an early stage teachers should have the opportunity to describe their circumstances to each other and then have time to discuss these accounts among themselves and digest the meaning before being asked to formalize their critical opinions. A few projects have held special evaluation conferences, but the majority prefer to include evaluative sessions in their conference programme, in which case the considerations outlined above need to be observed if useful opinion is to emerge. Those projects which have worked through the agencies of teacher writing groups, or which regularly hold meetings, can adopt the same methods but over a longer stretch of time, during which members may establish a knowledge of each other's backgrounds.

The difficulty of extracting opinion and feedback from discussion is partly that of recording the opinions as they are voiced. Tape recording of sessions seems an obvious method, but the technical problems can be daunting and transcription very costly in typists' time and effort. Furthermore, it is not always the case that a monolithic opinion emerges, and recording to supplement a written record of a secretary is probably the best compromise. At a conference of the Careers Education and Guidance Project, M. Cannon managed to feed back into the conference, while still in session, a summary of its views, graphically illustrated. Such efforts mean hard work but can amply repay the time expended by the re-focusing of discussion which is a consequence.

Interviews

The interview could justly be regarded as the basic technique of evaluation. Its uses are manifold, from subsidiary purposes of guiding the construction of attitude scales to being the foremost means of gathering opinions. It is worth emphasizing that most objective tests and observation schedules are based upon early interviewing and discussion, and that the survey by interview is a research methodology in its own right. But in the interview's very versatility lies a danger, for only the largest of projects have separate evaluation teams, and this means that, in most cases, the same person has to interview the same teacher in order to achieve different purposes, sometimes to organize, sometimes to evaluate. Inevitably, a definable relationship will emerge which inexorably and imperceptibly colours every dialogue.

An evaluator is neither in the situation of a therapist, patiently establishing *rapport* for the gaining of concealed information, nor in the position of a survey interviewer, making a single uninvolved contact to obtain neutral information. *Rapport* must be established, but it should be the *rapport* of fellow workers: sufficient to enable unfavourable attitudes to be expressed, sufficient even to allow the exploration of areas of difficulty in which the teacher might feel his competence to be under question. The Humanities Curriculum Project is a prime example of a project which was perceived as a challenge to teacher competence; but any project which suggests new methods of teaching rather than new materials gives rise to these uncertainties, and few projects would nowadays admit to be merely producing materials. On the other hand, if unbiased feedback is the aim, the establishment of *rapport* of a different kind can be fatal. Some teachers appear to enjoy adopting the role of a battle-scarred veteran being visited by a World War I general —tight-lipped and sceptical. Others use every meeting to underline their undying hostility to the whole notion of curriculum reform, especially as it seems to them to be keeping some people, who could be teaching, in comfortable jobs. An evaluator meets all these, and has to recognize the extent to which personality and circumstances influence judgement. A necessary safeguard is the cross-checking of these individual opinions against others.

In acknowledging that such judgements are made in the process of evaluation, it should not be assumed that an entirely subjective opinion is all that an interview can provide. The dangers of interviewer bias, failure to accept the aims of the interview, leading questions, etc. are thoroughly documented in the literature of sociology. (Standard handbooks are Hyman et al., 1962; Richardson, Dohrenwend and Klein, 1965; Sellitz et al., 1965.) By adopting the correct procedures; structuring the interview; establishing the necessary *rapport*; defining the information required; presenting the questions in a neutrally worded, standard fashion; supporting with non-committal cues; and cross-checking whatever information is obtained against other sources; an evaluator may ensure that contact with a general view of the reality of the situation is maintained. Sociology, in the person of Shipman (1972) has pointed out that the views of a project and its effect differ markedly as the viewpoint changes from that of project team members to trial teacher, to headteacher, to sponsor or even to the evaluator. It could be seriously misleading if data gathered from these differing—yet valid—viewpoints were to be unthinkingly merged.

Pupil opinion and reaction
'The customer is always right' says the adage. Who is the customer of curriculum reform—teacher, pupil, parent? Parents are rarely consulted, except in such activities as the Yorkshire West Riding's educational priority area scheme of pre-school visiting, which is not generally considered within the boundaries of curriculum development. In the minds of evaluators it would thus seem that parents are not customers, but pupils very definitely are. All the techniques described above for ascertaining teacher opinion have been used in soliciting pupil opinion of materials and methods. In addition, the *review of selected samples of pupil work* offers feedback data to the evaluator who wishes to confirm or deny hypotheses about the content and methods

used by teachers nominally following project direction. A project using this method is History 13–16. The general tendency of evaluators is to weigh pupil opinion less heavily than teacher opinion and sometimes, regrettably, to rely solely upon *teacher assessment* of pupil opinion, the safeguard of cross-checking being ignored. Teacher assessment of such matters is really based upon the teacher's observation of the pupil's manner of working, the pupil's reaction. Clearly this is not an unambiguous indication of the pupil's opinion of the work.

The worth of pupil opinion is limited by the pupil's restricted experience and often by the pupil's inability to express himself freely. The younger the child, the less his opinions are likely to be sought—understandably so. Teacher assessment of the reactions of children under eleven is heavily relied upon unless the methods of direct observation, described later (p. 72), are used. However, if other techniques could be developed, for instance Harlen's (1975) method of testing via the medium of closed loop film presentation or Kelly's (1955) repertory grid techniques, which have been used with young children, such reliance upon teacher reports might be avoided.

In contrast, at secondary level, in working through project materials, whether they be mathematical packages, guides to experimentation or language booklets, the pupils' responses are eagerly sought. 'How long did it take you?' 'Where precisely did the difficulty arise?' 'How interesting did you find this piece of work?' What is elicited is not solely opinion, but more an amalgam of opinion and reaction: not only what they think but also what they do, hence the heading to this subsection.

Feedback: general considerations
The designation of data as feedback implies an active intervention in a cycle of events, and such data must arrive in time to allow the active intervention to take place, even when this means that at times the data will be crude and highly selective. The evaluator must also confine his provision of data to those which will inform the proposed changes. He may put questions to teacher and pupils which are designed to free their responses and allow them to express opinions which they feel are worth airing but, unless the information is germane to the decision points ahead, he is foolish if he wastes precious time analysing such data and runs the risk of overloading the teacher and pupils. One project, for kindness' sake nameless, found that one-third of a term's course in one school had been given over to evaluation activities. The mistake was not repeated.

ATTAINMENT TESTING
This technique could, quite properly, come under the heading of a feedback technique. But the issues involved are wide and the method is not confined to the provision of feedback in the sense mentioned above. Attainment testing is

traditionally associated with the R, D and D (research, development and diffusion) model of curriculum development, in which the achievement of definable objectives is monitored. Borrowed, as the model is, from the world of science and technology, its application has been to the development of curricula in the sciences and mathematics. These subject areas most readily lend themselves to the specification of precise, testable objectives—often behaviourally formulated. But, in languages too, the use of attainment tests has been noticeable, for example in the Modern Languages Project, Bilingual Education and Attitudes to and Motivation for the Learning of Welsh and English in Wales.

In the early days of curriculum development it was thought that gains in attainment might be monitored by testing, so that the indisputable superiority of new methods and materials might be demonstrated. It is a matter of record that such hopes proved false. Especially in the introduction of programmed learning were these hopes frustrated, and cynics say that, ever since, evaluation has been seeking gains in every other way than the one that matters—attainment. It is true that attainment testing is unfashionable at present but here is not the place to repeat the arguments of the succeeding chapter. What does the technique of attainment testing offer? Potentially we may monitor changes in pupil attainment after 'exposure to the project'. But to show any comparative gains or losses involves two methods: control group procedures, and pre- and post-testing.

Control group procedures
Many others have argued the case for and against the use of control groups in evaluation. The basic difficulty in an educational context is that of supplying a control group which truly matches the teaching group which is being exposed to the new style of teaching. While matching on variables such as attainment levels, socio-economic background and school status may be achieved somewhat roughly in practice, the real difficulty lies in reproducing the enthusiasm factor and adequate similarity of aims in the control group. (For advice on when matching procedures are necessary see Ogilvie, 1974.) The enthusiasm, or innovative excitement, engendered by working with the project, which usually involves close attention to a teacher's viewpoint and difficulties, is likely to produce all the features of the well-known Hawthorne effect within the teaching group. This should not be regarded, as it often is, as a *defect* in the situation. In part, the aims of curriculum development include the exploitation of such enthusiasm effects throughout the teaching system. However, an evaluator will be hard pressed to obtain a control group which exhibits a similar enthusiasm.

There are ways around this difficulty for projects working on a large scale. Many projects, working with new teaching materials, collaborate with two very different samples of schools—trial schools and associated schools. The trial schools are officially visited and receive the full support of the project team in their use of the materials. The associated schools on the other hand, merely receive the project's materials, sometimes at cost price, and are not usually visited by the project. All they are asked to do in return for the materials is to submit questionnaire data on the effectiveness of the materials. An evaluator who visits such associated schools can find situations in which the project's aims and purposes are more truly represented than in some official trial schools. By sampling from these schools, which have not had the constant support of the project team, the equivalence of a control group situation may be constructed which allows to some extent for the factor of engendered enthusiasm. It is by then examining the reasons for differences in performance that an evaluator can estimate the potential of the project, unbiased by the effects of project support. In such comparisons, the use of carefully designed experiments which take advantage of sophisticated methods of statistical analysis offers a second method of handling the control group situation. The Integrated Science Project has employed control group procedures.

Pre- and post-testing

Pre- and post-testing, designed to measure changes—not always gains—in attainment due to new teaching styles has figured in the evaluations of projects concerned with mathematics, sciences and modern languages, e.g. Sixth Form Mathematics and Bilingual Education. It was at one time feared that simply by pre-testing one altered the situation, thereby invalidating the movement of scores shown by the post-test results. Research designed to test this possibility has not invariably supported this fear (Walch and Walberg, 1970). So the use of this technique, whether merely to reassure developers that their work is having some measurable effect—in which case careful controls are usually omitted—or whether in control group situations, has been freely adopted (e.g. by Science 5–13, Sixth Form Mathematics and Continuing Mathematics).

The crucial difficulty in applying attainment tests in these situations is that of being able to use a test appropriate to the situation. Where the subject area admits of definable items of knowledge, skill, evaluation, synthesis, etc. it is comparatively easy to form a pool of items from which the tests may be drawn. Each test should be recognized as a sample of items, however. And the pool of items must be adequately representative of the particular aims of the work under examination as well as adequate in size, if the test is to present a fair sample. This involves heavy time commitments for the construction of a test frame and the necessary content analysis and item analysis for two parallel tests to take place. It is rarely the case that existing standardized tests are appropriate either for the age range of pupils concerned or for the particular aims of the project within the subject area. Tests which are readily available are listed in some of the works mentioned below, in Buros (1972) and the regularly issued NFER catalogue. The construction of attainment tests is not lightly to be undertaken by a project evaluator. Standard works on the subject give details of the procedures which are necessary. (See Vernon, 1956; Anstey, 1966; Anastasi, 1968; Helmstadter, 1966; and Cronbach, 1960.)

Attainment testing in general
Attainment testing has fallen into disfavour in recent times in a manner that might be not unfairly attributed to changes in educational fashion. The aversion to such testing in an evaluation context is very misguided, as it relates to that no longer existing situation when such tests alone provided the criterion of successful innovation. Today, evaluators can set the results of attainment tests in a rich context of other information and this aversion to the use of tests is rarely justifiable. One should reflect that, on a different plane, attainment testing in the form of public examinations is an accepted evaluative measure for a large section of the population.

In fact, a number of projects at the higher secondary levels have become involved in the development of public examinations, working closely with the various examining boards concerned. The list of projects includes History 13–16, Geography 14–18, Sixth Form Mathematics and Integrated Science. This involvement potentially brings into use an external yardstick of attainment levels in the moderation procedures that examining boards apply. And, providing—as is the case in all instances so far—that the project team determines the relationship between the course and examination, there is the minimum of distortion to the course.

A growing difficulty in the blanket use of standardized attainment tests has sprung from the increase in mixed ability teaching groups in schools. Such organization is now common in the 11–14 age range within comprehensive schools over very many subjects. Teachers within the schools are still grappling with the problems of assessment that this form of organization brings, and experimenting with the various means of continuous assessment which involve variations on the use of profiles, measures of percentile progress within the year group, and close attention to rank ordering. There is an interest in the use of mastery tests which would determine when a pupil moves on through the course. These tests refer the pupil's attainment to pre-specified criteria of performance. They do not compare a pupil with the norms of his age group in the way that norm-referenced tests do.

Future use of attainment testing in schools will have to take account of such trends. Often, the information required by an evaluator does not justify the fine discrimination that standardized tests are constructed to supply. Crude levels of discrimination are often perfectly adequate for inter-group comparisons. It may be that there is a wealth of untapped comparative information to be uncovered by asking pupils, with proper guidance, to assess themselves, their abilities and the progress they have made on the course being investigated. It is an unshakeable tenet of clinical psychology that when a patient *feels* he is making progress, he *is* making progress.

ATTITUDINAL CHANGE AND MOTIVATION

Emphasis in present-day curriculum development is now firmly on the need to change attitudes of both teachers and pupils, if motivation within schools is to be improved and learning experiences made more effective. This emphasis has emerged as curriculum development has tried to cater for pupils in the lower ability ranges, whose situation has altered with the twin coming of large-scale comprehensive schools and RoSLA (the raising of the school leaving age). Evaulators therefore wish to know not only what the pupils' attitudes are towards these materials, this subject, etc. but, more important, whether attitudes have altered since the introduction of this particular development in the curriculum. Additionally, both the project developers and potential users wish to know which attitudes are favourable to the new approaches, and thereby enhance learning or even favour the associated changes of organization which teachers would find necessary. (See, for example, Sharp et al. (1973) on attitudes to Welsh and English.)

The central problem in assessing attitudes, and working in the affective domain generally, is that the link between professed attitudes—or even implicit attitudes—and actual behaviour is not straightforward. Researches have shown that attitudes measured by pen-and-paper tasks predict but poorly decisions made in real life. Actions are determined by group expectations, the individual's perception of the importance of the action for his own well-being, and other social considerations. Thus attitude information is unlikely to be useful in its own right, as with attainment test results; a context within which the information may be interpreted is essential.

The measurement of attitudes has traditionally involved the use of *attitude scales* on which individuals indicate their degree of agreement with various statements. Different kinds of scale have been evolved. Details of how such scales as those of Likert, Thurstone and Guttman may be constructed are given in standard texts such as Oppenheim (1966), Shaw and Wright (1967) and the works mentioned in the previous section. If such scales are to be adequately reliable, the initial pool of items required is very large, and the process of item refinement by judges or by analysis of internal self-consistency is very lengthy. The validity of a scale needs to be demonstrated as a separate exercise. This has always proved difficult, when it has been possible at all.

As is the case with attainment tests, it is unlikely that available attitude scales will be suitable for use in the context of a particular piece of curriculum development, though Alexander (1974) was able to use such an instrument in evaluating Nuffield Secondary Science. (See, however, Rennie, Lunzer and Williams (1974), where existing scales were unsuitable for evaluating a programme of social education.) Thus, the sample attitude scales given by Shaw and Wright (1967), who provide a description of the scale, details of the sample on which the scale is based, the kind of response required, the scoring, and comments on reliability and validity, are only marginally useful to an evaluator. The problem becomes one of constructing a suitable scale in the short time which most evaluators have available. Interim solutions can involve the use of *checklists* and *inventories* as described in Oppenheim. If time permits, the initial indications these give may form the basis for the construction of a Likert or Thurstone scale. Checklists and inventories are open to faking of responses and suffer from response sets. Their validity is generally regarded as low. But, even with comparatively crude indicators of attitude, useful results are forthcoming. For example, Williams (Health Education 5–13) found that the teachers in his working groups were far more in tune with the attitudes of the project team than had been previously suspected. This obviated needless attempts to influence already favourable attitudes towards health education of the form envisaged by the project.

Recently, two new approaches to the investigation of attitudes have grown in use. The *Osgood semantic differential* technique uses the concept of a semantic space to judge whether objects, persons, things or concepts are conceived as similar or dissimilar. Scales are used to define a semantic space. Commonly these are of bi-polar form, e.g. good–bad, strong–weak, active–passive; with seven-point scaling between the ends of the bi-polar scale. Teachers or pupils are invited to rate the item under consideration along each scale. If several items are rated on each scale in turn, it is possible to calculate the distance apart of the items in the semantic space. Items close together are considered to share attributes in the attitudes displayed. This technique rests upon a definition of meaning which depends upon the connotation of the language used. Much work has been done, and three main dimensions or axes have emerged: evaluation, potency and activity. Fleming (1973/4) has reported the use of the technique in an investigation of attitudes to mathematics apparently being affected by work on materials from the Mathematics for the Majority Continuation Project. Nottingham (1970) and Kitchen (1970) have also analysed pupil attitudes in this way.

The advantages of this technique spring from its indirectness and its generalizability. In *The Measurement of Meaning*, Osgood, Suci and Tannenbaum (1957) provide scales where the relevance to the main dimensions is well documented. However, there are strong drawbacks. The method can lack face validity in that, if asked to judge whether a piece of apparatus is sweet or sour, a person's credulity is somewhat stretched. The process of rating also tends to be tedious, and people often gibe at the bi-polar opposites supplied in the scales. The opposite of 'idle' is not 'busy' for everybody. By allowing the judgement of several items on the same scale to be made simultaneously, some of the tedium may be relieved. Although this means that the halo effect is then more likely to appear, it may be argued that, in matters of attitude and personal conceptualization, the halo effect is a legitimate reflection of a person's perceptions. There is also an assumption of equal interval scaling in the use of the rating scales, which is questionable in a region of personal judgement. For a discussion of the semantic differential's validity and reliability, see Warr and Knapper (1968, pp. 74–109).

From Kelly's personal construct theory (1955), there has evolved the use of a *repertory grid test* which was originally intended for clinical diagnosis. This overcomes the problem of poor face validity by allowing a person to label his own dimensions, which are then used for scaling. Judgements on the scales may be ranking, rating or dichotomous choices. Kelly and subsequent workers have found that, despite the use of a variety of labels, when analysed, many labels were being used to make essentially the same distinctions. The assumption is that, underlying these labels, there exist relatively few 'constructs' which are the determinants of the pattern of a person's thinking (Bannister and Mair, 1968).

Using their own labels increases people's acceptance of the technique, and presumably the approach to a truer reflection of a personal value system is enhanced in comparison to the public dictionary meanings which often have to be used in a semantic space. The repertory grid allows judgements by the evaluator of the similarity with which aspects of a project are viewed by the participants. In the information it supplies here, it resembles the semantic differential technique. But if every pupil or teacher may use his own individual scales, how may group attitudes be determined? The answer lies in using a mixture of 'supplied' and 'own' labels. It is also possible, if so wished, to mix in some of Osgood's dimensions. However, in practice Kelly's technique has not been widely used by evaluators although A. T. Ravenette, a clinical psychologist, has used the technique with quite young children, presenting pictures in order to elicit the necessary labels.

The methods of both Kelly and Osgood offer a speedy approach to the problem of determining attitudes when compared to the time necessary for conventional scale construction. They are difficult to fake because of their indirect nature, but the information they give is not strictly attitudinal. A view is offered of the pupil's or teacher's perceptions. There is still the difficulty of relation to behaviour, which bedevils the use of any attitudinal information. However, these methods provide an approach to the problem area of motivation through the possibilities they offer of investigation of the self-concept. Arguably, the pupil's self-concept is the greatest single determinant of his future progress. With the increasing interest in counselling and guidance in schools, interest in the effect the curriculum has on a pupil's self-awareness, self-concept and relationships with his peers will grow. Many projects in the humanities and social sciences have made the enhancement of a pupil's self-awareness one of their major aims.

Health Education 5–13 is such a project, currently tackling the details of assessing the effects of the project's efforts upon children's concepts of themselves, both as individuals and as members of several sociological groups. The project is proposing to use a number of sociometric devices. In addition to using attitude checklists and scales, and interviewing, the intention is to analyse pupil groupings by sociograms and relate the information provided by these pictures of pupil–pupil inter-relation to the kind of curriculum in health education appropriate to this age group and the social awareness revealed.

The investigation of attitude and motivation shows a marked division, both in the degree to which the investigation is pursued and in the kinds of technique which it is thought appropriate to apply to teachers as opposed to pupils. Pupils are considered fair game for the application of any technique, and the analysis is followed through in as much detail as possible. Teachers, on the other hand, are usually approached indirectly and their attitudes and motivation are more likely to be assessed on the basis of interviews rather than by answers to an attitude scale or semantic differential. There are valid reasons for this differentiation between pupils and teachers—reasons both psychological and sociological. Projects need to invite the co-operation of teachers as equals in an innovative venture. The fostering of such a spirit of co-operation is not easy if teachers are given the idea they are somehow under test.

But perhaps evaluators stray too far in their efforts to avoid giving the wrong impression. There are available a number of well-constructed tests of personality, notably those devised by R. B. Cattell and H. J. Eysenck, and evaluators would be providing useful information in a very generalizable form if the readiness of teachers to accept innovation could be judged in the light of these extensively validated tests.

DESCRIBING THE CURRICULUM CONTEXT AND PROCESSES

The term 'context' is very extensive, embracing not only those factors which operate outside the school to affect the education provided, but also those within the school. Thus, there are several levels on which the context may be considered to have effect. Within the school organization, at a general staffing level, difficulties may arise which affect the kind of curriculum offered to pupils. Limitations of choice within any one timetable are immediate examples, though the problems can be more subtle in nature. Co-operation between departments may adversely affect the outcomes of any integrated studies approach, and within the classroom itself the sheer availability of physical facilities, amount of space, adequate soundproofing, possession of equipment, etc. can have obvious effects. Furthermore, the quality of the teacher–pupil relationship, which may be recognized on a group level or in person-to-person contacts, is probably the major determining influence on effective learning, as this establishes the expectations of both parties.

The methods that evaluators have used to provide contextual descriptions and accounts of curricular processes reflect these different levels of possible interaction. Evaluators commonly describe the external features of the school environment; some use case studies which allow considerable latitude as to the level upon which the description centres, and within classrooms the application of direct observation, sometimes involving schedules and interactive measures, permits a close analysis of classroom processes. A general point worthy of consideration in attempts to provide such descriptions is whether this is best done by a participant or a non-participant observer.

External measures

Readers of evaluation reports expect some reference to the school's setting in a wider context, often a general description, reflecting the socio-economic area in which the school is placed and the intake of its pupils. It is possible to provide much more relevant information. Data such as the school type (e.g. comprehensive), sex, size, number of examination entrants, etc. is straightforwardly obtained and, with little additional research, it is possible to add the percentage of children applying to a school as their first choice, the sources from which the school draws its teaching staff, and accounts of how many of the school's outdoor activities involve real contact with the local community. The provision of such information enables the reader to interpret the evaluator's judgements, not only in a way which renders the interpretation more valid for his purposes, but also from a standpoint which may be unique to him. While such information is frequently gathered in the course of an evaluation, it is relatively rarely incorporated into the analysis and interpretation of findings. Some workers have tried to draw up a single-figure index of the school's educational setting on a sociological basis, following the lines drawn up by American workers describing college environments, but efforts in these directions have not proved very successful.

Case studies

From the fields of medicine and sociological studies the case study has grown into a major weapon in the armoury of evaluators, especially those who operate on a small scale in local studies. In use it can be very flexible. All the levels of context mentioned above are amenable to description in this way, and the great advantage of presenting a contextual description in this fashion is that it provides information about the inter-relationships involved. Additionally, a case study can reflect the perceived concerns of the author in a way which is often subconscious, but the more revealing because of this. The drawbacks to using a case study description are connected with its uncontrolled nature: at worst it may be too introspective and consequently unilluminating.

However, if the boundaries of a case study are clearly set down for the author, the drawbacks are minimized. The study may be longitudinal or sectional as required; it may be responsive to the demands of the situation and it could be focused on inter-personal relationships when these are important.

Close, Rudd and Plimmer, in a study published by the NFER (1974), based on work with the North West Regional Curriculum Development Project, provide accounts of different team teaching situations in anonymous schools. The accounts were written by teachers actively participating in the events, who describe not only classroom matters, but also problems of teacher co-operation and organization both in and out of the classroom. However, where different authors contribute, solutions are required to the problem of achieving comparable levels of approach and understanding. Editing may be necessary but it is a delicate affair, especially when dealing with inter-personal matters, and adequate standards of anonymity must be ensured if authors are not to moderate their comments for fear of offending colleagues.

Observation schedules
One lesson that curriculum developers have absorbed is that teachers show remarkable abilities to engulf new teaching ideas without necessarily altering their classroom behaviour. Observation has confirmed this as attention has focused upon happenings inside individual classrooms. Harlen describes in Chapter 3 how observation has moved from being based on casual observers to the use of pre-set schedules which categorize happenings on the basis of frequent sampling of activities. Commonly, an observer sits in the room and every few seconds or minutes, using a stopwatch, notes down what is happening at that time. The operation is usually repeated over several lessons, to provide a representative sample of events from which a teacher's profile may be constructed. This technique of recording classroom happenings has several potential uses but basically it enables changes to be registered when changes occur. This requires two things: first, adequate preliminary samples of behaviour, and secondly, categories on the schedule which reflect the changes in behaviour. The first requirement is a matter of organization, while the second is more subtle and leads to consideration of how schedules are produced.

The normal procedure for constructing a schedule starts with a number of suggestions based on hunches, interviews and previous experience. This process of sampling possibly relevant behaviours from the total universe of what goes on in a classroom has obvious limitations. Thus, users of schedules are required to demonstrate their reliability in use and the validity of the interpretations based on their use. Eggleston, Galton and Jones (1975) trained observers by the use of videotapes and were able to show high levels of inter-observer agreement in the study of science teaching. The validity of schedules has, however, often been built on the internal consistency of categories. This procedure can be highly dangerous, a fact emphasized by Hamilton and Delamont (1974). Schedules for observing teachers such as that of Hughes, described by Travers (1969), may have very high face validities—hers has categories such as 'sets standards', 'reprimands', 'demonstrates', etc.—but some external validation is essential to show that the behaviours observed actually correlate with and determine learning effectiveness.

Interaction schedules

Interaction schedules are similar to observation schedules both in construction and use, but aim to record sequences of behaviours in 'strings' of various lengths. Most often it is the linking of a pair of behaviours that is recorded—for instance, a teacher asks an open-ended question which is followed by a pupil request for more information—but the 'strings' may take any length. In recording interactions, the hope is to gain understanding at a deeper level than that afforded by isolated observations, so that, in principle, more may be said about patterns of teacher and pupil involvement in learning.

The practical difficulties that evaluators experience in preparing such schedules are the usual ones, lack of time and the heavy commitment of resources involved, for although many schedules have already been devised (see Medley and Mitzel, 1963; Simon and Boyer, 1967–72), projects often need to devise their own. Both the Extending Beginning Reading and Effective Reading Projects are doing so. There are additional difficulties because the interpretation of both observation and interaction schedules involves first an analysis of the structure and then a translation of the results. The analysis stage is often mathematical, and it is possible at this juncture to impose, unwittingly, a mathematical structure which need not be meaningful.

Schedules may be of two types, low inference or high inference. The low inference model records unambiguous data which do not require much judgement by the observer at time of recording, while high inference models demand that the observer makes judgements as to the intentions behind actions at the time of recording. Constructors of schedules often aim to produce 'objective' measures, but high inference schedules are easier to construct and can make use of the skills which may already exist. For example, if teachers are given adequate instruction, they may be trusted to use high inference methods because they readily understand teaching situations. Alexander (1974) found it possible to use experienced people in this way in the Nuffield Secondary Science evaluation.

It is remarkable that the use of both observation and interaction schedules has not been primarily directed at describing the context of learning as such. Observers and users have tried to establish cause-and-effect relationships in the classroom, concentrating more on processes. This is to ignore the wealth of information that such methods can provide. Even when clear relationships have not been established, data obtained from a schedule may still provide invaluable background descriptions.

Participant observation

One might well argue that the only people qualified to describe adequately what goes on within a school or classroom are the participants. The onlooker, armed with interview or observation schedule, may see most of the game, but it could be just those aspects hidden from his perception by the inevitable disturbance of his presence that are the critical ones. On the other hand there is, in all the social sciences, a long tradition of mistrusting the accounts of those involved in situations as actors. Unconscious motivations, self-justification and *post hoc* rationalizations can all operate to bias such accounts, but what other basis exists for anyone to show the insights of those actually involved in the reality of teaching without becoming prey to these same biases ?

From sociology and anthropology evaluators have borrowed a technique which offers the possibility of being both participant and observer. In sociology, the method has been used to study inner city street gangs and extreme political and religious groups by observers who, for a period of time, become members of the gang or group in order to observe the situation from the inside. In a school, as Nash (1973) describes, it involves virtually becoming one of the teaching staff: taking lessons, accompanying children on trips and attending staff meetings. Jenkins (1973) used the technique in evaluating the Integrated Studies Project. In a sense, it is an attempt to skate safely on wet, thin ice. If the evaluator stays on the dry, firm area and merely observes systematically, he has failed to test the water. If, on the other hand, he plunges through and becomes immersed in the situation, forgetting the business of systematic observation, that too rates as failure, rendering suspect the data gathered.

It is altogether a finely judged business, and unfortunately those reading the report of an evaluation which has used this method have very little to guide them on how successfully the evaluator judged it. Some clues lie in the kinds of data obtained. If such data are purely anecdotal, the chances are that the evaluator was more participant than observer; if there are too many pencil-and-paper tests, the chances are that the evaluator was never truly accepted as a participant by the other teachers or the pupils. However, even granting these difficulties, there is little doubt that, when successful, participant observation offers unrivalled insights into the context of educational change.

OTHER TECHNIQUES AND METHODOLOGIES

So far, it has been possible to confine attention to the techniques and methods used in evaluation rather than the methodologies and styles of working that different evaluators espouse in different circumstances. But it is now necessary to examine three particular methodologies because of the different techniques they call upon. They may be referred to as intrinsic evaluation, the provision of an evaluation data bank and evaluation as the writing of history.

Techniques of intrinsic evaluation
There is a hidden stage of evaluation for most curriculum development projects which comes at the time when their feasibility is under scrutiny—particularly when a funding body is considering the project in proposed form. Answers are sought to such questions as:

Are the aims of this project the right ones to pursue ?
Are the aims acceptable to teachers ?
Is the content suitable for the target population of pupils and consistent with the aims ?
Do the envisaged methods of teaching fit the content and aims ?

Normally the funding body applies intuitive methods to answering such queries, but in recent projects attempts have been made to carry this process consciously into the project's life span.

The techniques which have evolved and are still evolving in this connexion vary a great deal. Sometimes they comprise no more than a conscious effort to keep the output of the project within a framework such as the Piagetian developmental psychology followed by Science 5–13 or the linguistic theories adhered to by the Language in Use Project. The judges of the project's success in such endeavours have been predominantly within the project team itself, and this has evident drawbacks. Intimate involvement in the development process makes unbiased judgement difficult and, after some time together, project teams experience a convergence of patterns of thought which may miss ideas and criticisms that an outsider could contribute. Projects have deliberately set up *panels of outside experts* to advise on the content of their materials.

The Sixth Form Mathematics Project invited a group of experts from biology, physics, economics and other disciplines to help in the development of the project's draft materials, which were also tested in trial schools. The project has been developing the use of mathematical modelling of hypothetical situations, the power of mathematics being used to analyse each situation when in model form. The expert advisers meet two to three times each year to be brought up to date with the progress of the project and its thinking. They are asked to examine the materials, identify errors, provide additional examples of situations amenable to simple modelling in mathematical terms, suggest improvements, provide references from which the background information on the real-life situations may be supplied to pupils, and generally comment on the overall acceptability of the problem situations used in the draft texts. Between the meetings, members of the advisory panel may be consulted individually about problems concerning their speciality, and specific problems may be brought to their notice for comment on prepared forms. The Humanities Curriculum Project made use of a similar group of people called 'critical friends'.

This kind of intrinsic evaluation of the project's materials at a formative stage was also used in the Inter-University Biology Teaching Project. In addition to the evaluation trials, two groups of experts in biology were invited to aid in the preparation of materials. One group was made up of biologists who were at Sussex University, the base of the project. They were called upon whenever expert opinion was required at the writing stage. Other experts, external to Sussex, formed the second group who commented on the subject matter of the materials on the basis of supplied drafts. The common feature to both these methods of involving experts is the informality of much of the exchange of comment. There was also a clear realization that the projects were open to change on the basis of the comments received. This state of affairs might well be more difficult to achieve if the subject area under development were not mathematics or science, or if the organization were not centrally based, although projects such as Mathematics for the Majority Continuation Project, which use teacher writing groups, could exchange materials for this kind of scrutiny before putting them on trial in schools.

The technique of *content analysis*, introduced during the sixties from the field of literature studies and used chiefly in social psychology, appears suitable for application in an intrinsic evaluation context but has not been employed to any great extent. The problems underlying this lack of interest appear to centre upon the need for precise specification of criteria by which the written content may be judged. The possible difficulties of determining criteria for establishing how far a text encourages 'enhancement of the self-concept' perhaps show why content analysis has until now been reserved for more specific matters such as vocabulary levels and readability. However, recent work at Sussex University (Eraut et al., 1975) looks more promising and has already produced a detailed analysis of the 'Ladybird' reading scheme.

The Careers Education and Guidance Project has been in a position to make use of some of these methods. The project has been providing materials for careers teaching in the form of a newspaper entitled *Framework*. The reading level of the text has been monitored by word difficulty counts. In a separate use of the methods of content analysis, the project evaluator M. Cannon has been coding key phrases and ideas contained in taped interviews with teachers and the extra comments gathered on teacher opinion questionnaires. When a batch of questionnaires is received, a small sample is examined and the comments given an initial crude coding. For example, comments may concern the value of the materials to the teacher, the enjoyment shown by the pupils, the interest shown, and other broad categories which may then be subdivided at a later stage. This method avoids the straitjacket of predetermined categories, which could easily misrepresent the actual opinions received in response to an individual issue of *Framework*. But the depth of analysis cannot be great because of the balance that the evaluator has to maintain between the time and effort expended and the need to provide information that appears sufficiently valid for the writers to be prepared to alter their approach on its basis. The validity of a more detailed and theoretical analysis of opinions at a covert level would be difficult to demonstrate.

These emergent techniques provide the tools of intrinsic evaluation, but the possible effects of this kind of evaluation must be limited by the present patterns of organization and funding of curriculum development, in which the basic aims and premises of a project are unlikely to be mutable. The whole situation militates against this sort of flexibility, because a funding body likes to know in advance how its money is going to be spent. Steering groups and consultative committees are deliberately set up with one of their main purposes being to ensure that the work proceeds in promised directions. Here the necessary intrinsic evaluation has to take place even before funding is assured, usually occurring during the funding body's judgemental deliberations.

An evaluation data bank

Careers Education and Guidance, as well as providing examples of content analysis, is the scene for a distinctive approach to the gathering of evaluative data. All the quantifiable data concerning schools, teachers, classes and pupils, gathered from a variety of sources—mainly, but not exclusively, from questionnaires—is being coded in a form amenable to computer handling. This body of information will then be a data base designed to serve a number of possible future uses.

Although all the data must be quantifiable in order to fit this system, they are not all objective. By including details of school size, sex and internal organization alongside judgements on the successful use of the project's outputs, the potential is created for subsequent analysis, perhaps involving clustering methods, which would allow identification of the facilitating factors which promote innovative change within schools and classes. If carried out with a large enough number of schools, the extraction of subsamples would make it possible to see, for example, whether schools with an officially designated 'head of careers' accepted the project's aims any more consistently than schools with no separate provision for the organization of careers education. A similar analysis is reported by Harlen (1975).

Of course, this approach to analysing and interpreting the data is supplemented by extensive use of contextual information gathered from interviews and other less quantifiable sources. It merely reflects a systematic approach to the problem of handling the wealth of data that an evaluator may obtain with relative ease. The approach also highlights the dual problem of sampling which confronts all evaluators. What sample of information is most pertinent and what sample of situations should be examined? The provision of a data base does not solve these problems. It does sharpen the thinking on what data are worthy of inclusion and it does, potentially, allow sampling from the whole range of 'experimental' situations, although this can become expensive of time and money.

In practice, the method has drawbacks which spring from the twin problems mentioned above. Schools do drop out from the project. This need not be harmful if all the data for that school are already in the bank, but this is not normally the case because collection of data takes time and some data worthy of inclusion are not available until late in a project's life span. The judgement of what data to include involves the second major drawback. While it is possible to leave space in the data coding for later inclusion of new data or data now realized to be useful, but the time this happens it may be impossible to gather the information from all schools without intolerable nuisance. In short, the drawbacks of a data bank are the holes in the data that inevitably appear.

Evaluation and the history of a project
At least a marginal interest for evaluators during the course of a project should lie in ensuring that an adequate historical record of events is preserved. In the future such a record will serve as a valuable context within which judgement may be made of the success of different types of curriculum development. In a sense, this work is justifiable as preparing for a possible summative evaluation at a later date. Even if a summative evaluation of the project's teaching methods and/or materials never takes place, the basis will still be laid for future historians to compare different forms of curriculum development and their effects.

An adequate historical record would include copies of important documentation, discussion documents, lists of trial institutions and key personnel. A central record would be a carefully kept diary of events, visits and conferences, annotated to indicate when important decisions were made. The keeping of such a diary is not easy, and as an evaluator is often a traveller by the very demands of his occupation, a team member may have to accept this duty. Even then, there may remain uncertainty as to how and when certain key decisions were made. But, for example, if later judges are to know whether unsuccessful dissemination activities were the result of decisions to involve more trial schools being taken too late, the basic information must be provided. Such activities as are required in providing for future historians do not involve difficult applications of delicate techniques; rather, they involve the evaluator in increasing the awareness of others as to the need for adequate documentation and record-keeping. Within the busy life of a project, this is a technique in itself.

CONSTRAINTS AND OTHER PROBLEMS

In this section, attention is given to the constraints which may affect an evaluator's choice and use of techniques, and to a number of persistent problems which face evaluators. These latter problems, of sampling, of interpretation of results and of possible distortion effects, are matters on which inexperienced readers of evaluation reports have a right to expect guidance. The understanding of an evaluator's account may be radically altered if the constraints under which he laboured and the difficulties of interpreting the available information are properly appreciated.

Constraints
Before an inquirer is fully able to judge the correct application of appropriate techniques in an evaluation, consideration must be given to the often major constraints which operate to restrict an evaluator's choice. In Chapter 2 Tawney says much on this. Suffice it here to illustrate by reference to the situation in which an evaluator is commissioned to obtain only certain sets of information within a given time scale. This was the experience of P. S. Clift, who was given three months to carry out an evaluation of the Primary Pilot Project—a new method of teaching science and mathematics through the medium of English language in Singaporean schools. His brief rested on the basis that the inquirers were already convinced of the advantages that such a change would confer in the realms of attitudinal change and other contextual matters. All that was sought was an assurance that attainment levels in schools exposed to the new method were not being lowered. The twin external restraints were in the kind of evaluative evidence which was required and in the time allowed.

Time is a constant constraint. It may not only operate as a factor in this external fashion but also be an implicit constraint upon the use of techniques. Restrictions on an evaluator's choice of techniques are readily appreciated when they spring from the nature of the subject area of the curriculum under review. It is expected, in the examination of mathematics or sciences and, to a surprising extent, languages—all of which share a cummulative structure— that attainment testing by objective tests will figure prominently. It is less obvious that available time alone may often make it impossible to construct measures of attitude which would be adequately valid and reliable in use. There is yet a third way in which evaluators must pay time its due; the careful timing of their attempts to secure information. It is not unknown for an evaluator to realize too late that the possibility of pre- and post-testing being mobilized as a technique rests upon the pre-tests being applied *before* the sequence of instruction begins.

Self-imposed constraints may also exist as the result of the general approach or style of evaluation adopted. In this area evaluators reveal their personalities and origins. For the techniques of evaluation are, almost without exception, borrowed from other disciplines. This is inevitable. Curriculum development ranges across many disciplines, not solely in terms of the school subject areas being developed but also in relation to the ever-widening range of viewpoints which are focused upon schools. Psychologists, who for over half a century have produced theories of learning and supplied a range of psychometric methods, have in the last fifteen years been joined by sociologists, economists and systems analysts in examining the effects of education. The much adapted methods of clinical psychiatry may be detected alongside anthropological approaches, and the resulting data could be subjected to statistical analysis in a fashion borrowed from biological taxonomy; such is the hybrid nature of evaluation methodology.

Few evaluators—if any—have a training in all these disciplines; those mentioned above are not an exhaustive list, and it must be admitted that there is a tendency for an evaluator, faced with a choice of possible techniques, to favour those he knows well. The difference may be no more than a slight preference. Asked to obtain teacher opinion of new teaching materials, the sociology-trained evaluator may elect to do so by interviewing the teachers, the psychometrist may prefer to use a questionnaire. In reality, both would probably be used to provide cross-checks, but some kind of preference would exist and there still might be a tendency for the psychometrician's question-naires to be thought of as providing 'hard' and the sociologist's interviews as providing 'soft' data. No value judgement is intended here, although others seem to make them. Soft pillows make poor foundations and bricks make poor beds. The skill required is to find the correct technique when only one is appropriate and to arrange for cross-checking when more than one method may be applied. Here it suffices to draw attention to these differing attitudes to measurement methodology. Such attitudes underlie many evaluation reports, and the interested reader should bear in mind the effects that the attitudes of an evaluator can have as constraints on the choice and use of techniques. In the context of constraints one should include the unspoken agreement already referred to (p. 70) that no overt attempt be made to measure the personality of individual teachers. Although that particular constraint is conceivably elastic in certain circumstances, the agreement appears inviolable in the matter of measuring the competence of individual teachers.

Sampling

Evaluators very often lack control over the choice of the range of situations in which the curriculum development being evaluated takes place. This may be because the evaluator is a late-comer to the scene and is thus unavailable to offer advice on the selection of trial schools. More often, it is because LEAs traditionally select the schools to participate, and the basis of their selection rarely involves the strictures of educational research. This may lead to not having a single sex boys' comprehensive school, for example, involved in the project. Information relevant to up to one-twelfth of all comprehensive schools would then be unobtainable.

The traditional answer to this problem of the uncontrolled nature of the experimental situation has been to use large samples and apply multivariate methods of analysis. Harlen (p. 49) cites one project's solution. However, if a co-operative LEA's help can be enlisted, carefully designed experiments can be mounted to investigate specific issues. The project on Extending Beginning Reading has used an elaborately designed analysis of variance within a small sample of schools to obtain key information on the types of reading error children are prone to at different ages after leaving an initial reading scheme behind them.

The notion of what constitutes an 'adequate' sample in the context of curriculum development is a tangled one. Whenever the intention is to ascertain numerical levels, obtained by tests or scales, and supply statements about the attendant error, the requirements of classical sampling theory apply. The samples have to be quite large if the accuracy is to be sufficient for useful conclusions to be drawn, because of the need for randomness in the sampling procedure. Formulae exist for calculating the required sample size in these circumstances (see Hays, 1970, and Cochran, 1963). On the other hand, curriculum development focuses upon the quality of interactions between teachers and pupils, and it is not always necessary to quote numerical levels or give standard errors within the population. The need is for information which is generalizable, and reveals cause-and-effect relationships. The question of how many instances should be considered before being able to draw reliable inferences is not then answerable by statistical theory. Educational experience and judgement must be brought to bear.

If adequately selected samples are required, an evaluator, unless skilled already, should seek the advice of experts in the subject. A useful primer on the subject is provided by Butcher (1966), and good introductions to experimental design in an educational context may be found in Lewis (1968) and in Campbell and Stanley (1963). Many projects, however, do not work in a way that could profit from this rigorous approach. In this case, it is usually sufficient to ensure that the schools in which the project's development is to take place include adequate numbers of every type likely to be of interest in the way they respond to the innovation. It is not sufficient to have just one of each different type and, if it is thought that school type, size and sex might affect the outcomes, then the number of schools necessary for a project to work with soon becomes quite large. In general, projects work with too few schools to provide an adequate variety of situations in which outcomes may be evaluated.

Interpretation and distortion
Many readers may already be working in the field of education and are thus

aware of the inherent difficulty of assigning effects to causes in an educational setting. At an early stage in Communication Skills in Early Childhood, it was proposed that the project's attempts to promote awareness in teachers of the range of language available to young children should be evaluated by applying content analysis to videotape recordings of teacher group meetings, made at one of the first meetings and again at a later stage in the project. An objection was raised. How would it be known that any changes observed were due to the project's intervention? The reply came. What else could the changes be due to? This kind of Sherlock Holmes—when you have eliminated all else, Watson—approach is often resorted to. It is not necessarily misleading, but it does depend upon the fertility of the imagination. Evaluators should prefer to depend upon the reliability and validity of their techniques. In the preceding sections these aspects of the various evaluative techniques have for the most part been passed over, because in their technical sense such aspects receive more than adequate coverage in the standard texts mentioned, and because this technical sense is only appropriate with some of the evaluation methods used.

If it is possible to apply attainment tests, it is fitting to know the test/re-test reliability of the instrument used and even to appreciate that the technical reliability of tests may be calculated in many different ways (see Nuttall and Willmott, 1972). But readers of evaluators' reports really want to know whether the data gathered in other ways are reliable too. Would the same information have been obtained if a woman had replaced the male evaluator? Would the same kinds of outcome described in this middle-sized mixed junior high school be obtained in any similar school? The concept of reliability being applied here is very different from the restricted technical sense in which it may be applied to tests, attitude scales and observers using observation schedules. When data have been obtained informally, it is not always possible to offer reassurance of adequate reliability even in the technical sense. Evaluators should be ready to admit this and to offer instead the amalgam of reliability and validity data which inquirers often have in mind. The validity of even informally obtained views is open to confirmation if a proper programme of cross-checking has been incorporated into the evaluation and the context of events is adequately delineated.

A few words of warning are also due on the possibly distorting effect which choice of evaluative techniques may have on the curriculum development being evaluated. This danger is not likely to be so real now that a range of evaluative methods is available. But certainly, in the days when outcomes and objectives had had to be specified in behavioural terms before an evaluator would grant a team member rest, there is little doubt that distortion was sometimes a result of the desire to apply objective measures of behavioural change. Perhaps the curriculum developers of that time—just a few years back—developed skills in fostering the subjectively experienced changes that were really sought, while the testers carried on looking for the penny under the lamp-posts of their tests because that was where the light was. Distortion of aims is possible in any project if an evaluator is too firmly wedded to certain methods. Evaluation is a service industry and must remain so.

A FRAMEWORK FOR CHOICE

Towards the beginning of this chapter three groups of readers were imagined: those who wish to know what substance lies behind the title of evaluation, those who wish to judge the information offered in an evaluation report, and those who may wish to select appropriate techniques for use. Having read this far, the first of those three groups should now be saying: 'Is that all there is to it; does evaluation comprise the application of a variety of techniques filched from the purses of psychometricians, sociologists and others?' Such a conclusion is not far wrong, provided allowance is made for the complexities of the situation and the peculiar concerns of evaluation in an educational context.

The latter two groups should now find themselves with a common framework. They both wish to judge which techniques ought to be applicable, the readers in order to answer the three questions with which this chapter started, and the potential evaluators in order to apply the techniques. Their thought processes should follow the same path. First, they should consider the area of the curriculum which is the focus of the development. Is it an area of standardized normative achievement in science, mathematics and, to a lesser extent, modern languages—or is it a repository of subjective educative thinking? The next step should be a joint consideration of the aims of the project and the aims of the evaluation. Little has been said explicitly on this, but curricular aims which have been properly formulated frequently indicate their means of assessment. The aims of the evaluation should be similarly clear. Is it to raise questions or to provide answers? Is it formative, serving the project workers during the development of ideas and materials, or summative, attempting to judge the eventual effects of the project when released to the world at large and to inform potential customers? This will decide the range and type of data to be collected. Feedback techniques figure in most evaluations but are the other interests represented in the evaluation outline? Many evaluations, for good reasons, forego attempts to measure attainment. What are the constraints which have been applied to this evaluation? And when the appropriate techniques have been selected, perhaps mentally for later use, it is time to estimate the limits of reliability and validity that those particular methods imply. What does the evaluation owe most to—the world of psychometrics, sociometrics or phenomenology?

The reader of a report would here search for information on the sampling methods used and details of the interpretations offered him; an intending evaluator would be by now just starting to grapple with providing answers for future readers.

5 Evaluation as illumination[*]

Malcolm Parlett and David Hamilton

Although innovation is now a major educational priority, the developing field of evaluation has so far lacked coherent frames of reference. Dominant among rival schools of thought is the classical, or 'agricultural-botany' approach deriving from experimental and mental testing traditions in psychology. It can be criticized as expensive, cumbersome and inadequate when applied to education. Illuminative evaluation, rooted in social anthropology, seeks rather to describe and interpret, and takes account of the contexts in which educational innovations must function. Central concepts are the instructional system and the learning milieu. Within a three-stage framework of observation, further inquiry and explanation, the investigation's focus is progressively reduced and concentrated on the issues that emerge. The authors discuss the organization and methods, problems and possibilities of illuminative evaluation, and relate this approach to decision-making.

INTRODUCTION

Innovation is now a major educational priority. For nearly two decades it has expanded and proliferated. It absorbs increasing sums of public and private money. Its impact is felt throughout the world (see, for example, the Organisation for Economic Co-operation and Development's series of reports (1971) reviewing developments in member countries). Curricula are re-structured, new devices introduced, forms of teaching permutated. But decisions to change are more than educational: questions of politics, ideology, fashion and finance also intervene. More recently—to aid decision-making—innovation has been joined by evaluation. Increasingly, committees and foundations fund evaluation studies as an integral part of curriculum projects. Like inno-

* This chapter is an edited version of 'Evaluation as illumination: a new approach to the study of innovatory programs', Occasional Paper 9 of the Centre for Research in the Educational Sciences, University of Edinburgh. The prepation of this paper was supported by a grant from the Nuffield Foundation.

vation itself, evaluation has rapidly developed a legitimacy and importance of its own: professional journals have been launched and research centres established. The 'evaluator' has emerged as a new and influential figure. In short, both innovation and evaluation have become 'big science' (Price, 1963).

As a new field, the evaluation of curriculum projects has encountered a wide range of problems, both theoretical and methodological. Current concerns include the roles of evaluation (Scriven, 1967); the neutrality of the evaluator (Caro, 1971); the value of classroom observation (Light and Smith, 1970); the function of formative evaluation (Smith, 1971); the use of objectives (Popham et al., 1969); and the value of long-term studies (Caro, 1971). Much of this debate has been monitored by the American Educational Research Association's monograph series on curriculum evaluation (published by Rand McNally from 1967). Confusion is engendered as rival proposals, models and terminologies are voiced and then rapidly countered. As a developing field of study, evaluation proceeds in the absence of coherent or agreed frames of reference.

More generally within educational research, two distinct paradigms* or schools of thought can be discerned. Each has its own strategies, foci and assumptions. Dominant is the classical or 'agricultural-botany' paradigm (Parlett, 1972),† which utilizes a hypothetico-deductive methodology derived from the experimental and mental testing traditions in psychology. Almost all evaluation studies have resided within this traditional paradigm.

More recently, a small number of empirical studies have been conceived outside the agricultural-botany framework, and relate instead to social anthropology, psychiatry and participant observation research in sociology (e.g. Henry, 1971; Jackson, 1968; Young, 1971). Such research can be thought of as representing a second and contrasting paradigm, with a fundamentally different research style and methodology from that of mainstream educational research. This chapter outlines an approach to evaluation that belongs to this alternative, 'social-anthropology' paradigm (Parlett, 1972).

TRADITIONAL EVALUATION AND THE
AGRICULTURAL-BOTANY PARADIGM

The most common form of agricultural-botany evaluation is presented as an assessment of the effectiveness of an innovation by examining whether or not it has reached required standards on pre-specified criteria. Students—rather

* 'Paradigm' is a term used by T. S. Kuhn (1970) as an overarching concept similar in meaning to 'world view', 'philosophy' or even 'intellectual orthodoxy'. A paradigm prescribes problem fields, research methods, and acceptable standards of solution and explanation for the academic community it embraces.
† The designation 'agricultural-botany' is not fortuitous. Many of the statistical and experimental techniques used in educational research were originally developed (e.g. by R. A. Fisher) for use in agricultural experimentation.

like plants—are given pre-tests (the seedlings are weighed or measured) and then submitted to different experiences (treatment conditions). Subsequently, after a period of time, their attainment (growth or yield) is measured to indicate the relative efficiency of the methods (fertilizers) used. Studies of this kind are designed to yield data of one particular type, i.e. 'objective' numerical data that permit statistical analyses. Isolated variables like IQ, social class, test scores, personality profiles and attitude ratings are codified and processed to indicate the efficiency of new curricula, media or methods.

For instance, within this framework Lindvall and Cox have argued that the 'effectiveness' of an innovation is 'determined' by the answers to four basic questions (1970, pp. 5–6):

(1) What goals should the program achieve?
(2) What is the plan for achieving these goals?
(3) Does the operating program represent a true implementation of the plan?
(4) Does the program, when developed and put into operation, achieve the desired goals?

At face value these questions seem reasonable. But they embody problematic assumptions. For example, projects rarely have clearly specified and commonly agreed 'desired goals'. Measurement of 'goal achievement' is never unequivocal. To speak of a 'true implementation' is utopian, even nonsensical in terms of educational practice.

Again, within this framework, it has been proposed (Light and Smith, 1970, p. 18) that

. . . the search for (compensatory) programs which are working well should become a three-step procedure:

(1) First, locate the best recreatable centers, employing techniques which use estimates of average random variation. This will require analysis of variance, followed by multiple comparison procedures.
(2) Estimate, separately, the impact of random factors upon only the best-performing centers.
(3) Use this selective estimate of random variations to test whether these best centers are out-performing chance, and are worth recreating.

This evaluation is based purely on numerical results; no other data would be collected or eligible for consideration.

Recently, however, there has been increasing resistance to evaluations of this type. The objections are developed more extensively in Guttentag (1971), Stake (1973), MacDonald (1971), Messick (undated), Taylor (1971) and Parlett (1972). The most notable shortcomings may be briefly summarized as follows.

(a) Educational situations are characterized by numerous relevant parameters. Within the terms of the agricultural-botany paradigm, these must be randomized using very large samples, or otherwise strictly controlled. The former approach entails a major data collection exercise and is expensive in time and resources. It also runs counter to the need, widely acknowledged, for evaluation before large-scale application rather than after it. The latter procedure—of strict control—is rarely followed. To attempt to simulate laboratory conditions by 'manipulating educational personnel' is not only dubious ethically, but also leads to gross administrative and personal inconvenience. Even if a situation could be so unnervingly controlled, its artificiality would render the exercise irrelevant: rarely can 'tidy' results be generalized to an 'untidy' reality. Whichever approach is used, there is a tendency for the investigator to think in terms of 'parameters' and 'factors' rather than of 'individuals' and 'institutions'. Again, this divorces the study from the real world.

(b) 'Before and after' research designs assume that curriculum projects undergo little or no change during the period of study. This built-in premise is rarely upheld in practice. Yet it remains fundamental to the design, constraining the researchers from adapting to the changed circumstances that so frequently arise. To take an example, during the long-term evaluation of a Swedish individualized mathematics project (IMU, see Larsson, 1973), teachers who wished to transfer students from one class to another were actively discouraged by the evaluator from doing so, on the grounds that it would render inter-class comparisons invalid. Teachers also requested separate diagnostic tests for less able children. But again this educational need was subordinated to the evaluator's requirements. The British evaluation (Downing, 1967) of the initial teaching alphabet (i.t.a.), set up to compare pupil progress with i.t.a. and with traditional orthography (t.o.) over a five-year period, provides a second example. Early before and after test results indicated that a major educational difficulty was faced by children transferring from i.t.a. to t.o. But nothing was done to focus attention on this problem: the research die had already been cast.

Thus, traditional evaluation may even have a deleterious effect on the project itself, by discouraging new developments and re-definitions in midstream. Longitudinal studies, for these reasons, rarely can serve an effective 'formative' or cybernetic function. Moreover, as the pre-specification of parameters, by definition, occurs at the outset, variables which emerge during the study are likely to be left out of the analysis. In an extreme case this neglect of 'new' variables may negate an entire evaluation study. After criticism that it had not controlled for the Hawthorne effect, the i.t.a. experiment was re-started after two years.

(c) The methods used in traditional evaluations impose artificial and arbitrary restrictions on the scope of the study. For instance, the concentration on seeking quantitative information by objective means can lead to neglect of other data, perhaps more salient to the innovation, which are disregarded as being 'subjective', 'anecdotal', or 'impressionistic'. However, the evaluator is likely to be forced to utilize information of this sort if he is satisfactorily to explain his findings, weight their importance and place them in context.

(d) Research of this type, by employing large samples and seeking statistical generalizations, tends to be insensitive to local perturbations and unusual effects. Atypical results are seldom studied in detail. Despite their significance for the innovation, or possible importance to the individuals and institutions concerned, they are ironed out and lost to discussion.

(e) Finally, this type of evaluation often fails to articulate with the varied concerns and questions of participants, sponsors and other interested parties. Since classical evaluators believe in an 'objective truth' equally relevant to all parties, their studies rarely acknowledge the diversity of questions posed by different interest groups.

These points suggest that applying the agricultural-botany paradigm to the study of innovations is often a cumbersome and inadequate procedure. We are not, of course, arguing here against the use of experimental longitudinal or survey research methods as such. Rather, for the reasons suggested, we submit that they are usually inappropriate, ineffective or insufficient for project evaluation purposes. Too often, the evaluation falls short of its own tacit claims to be controlled, exact and unambiguous. Rarely, if ever, can educational projects be subject to strict enough control to meet the design's requirements. Innovations, in particular, are vulnerable to manifold extraneous influences. Yet the traditional evaluator ignores these. He is restrained by the dictates of his paradigm to seek generalized findings along pre-ordained lines. His definition of empirical reality is narrow. One effect of this is that it diverts attention away from questions of educational practice towards more centralized bureaucratic concerns.

ILLUMINATIVE EVALUATION AND
THE SOCIAL-ANTHROPOLOGY PARADIGM

Although traditional forms of evaluation have been criticized in this way, little attempt has been made to develop alternative models. The model described here, *illuminative evaluation*,* takes account of the wider contexts in which educational innovations function. Its primary concern is with description and interpretation rather than measurement and prediction (for three published reports which approach the style advocated here see Hanley et al., 1969; Smith and Pohland, 1971; Parlett and King, 1971). It stands

---

* The term 'illuminative evaluation' is drawn from Trow (1970). The approach to evaluation described here grew out of research at Massachusetts Institute of Technology in association with B. R. Snyder and M. J. Kahne (see Parlett, 1969).

unambiguously within the alternative anthropological paradigm. The aims of illuminative evaluation are to study the innovatory project: how it operates; how it is influenced by the various school situations in which it is applied; what those directly concerned regard as its advantages and disadvantages; and how students' intellectual tasks and academic experiences are most affected. It aims to discover and document what it is like to be participating in the scheme, whether as teacher or pupil; and, in addition, to discern and discuss the innovation's most significant features, recurring concomitants, and critical processes. In short, it seeks to address and to illuminate a complex array of questions (Trow, 1970, p. 302):

Research on innovation can be enlightening to the innovator and to the whole academic community by clarifying the processes of education and by helping the innovator and other interested parties to identify those procedures, those elements in the educational effort, which seem to have had desirable results.

The paradigm shift entailed in adopting illuminative evaluation requires more than an exchange of methodologies: it also involves new suppositions, concepts and terminology. Central to an understanding of illuminative evaluation are two concepts: the 'instructional system' and the 'learning milieu'.

The instructional system
Educational catalogues, prospectuses and reports characteristically contain a variety of formalized plans and statements which relate to particular teaching arrangements. Each of these summaries can be said to constitute or define an instructional system; and includes, say, a set of pedagogic assumptions, a new syllabus, and details of techniques and equipment. This 'catalogue description' is an idealized specification of the scheme: a set of elements arranged to a coherent plan. Despite their immense variation, the Dalton Plan, performance contracting, programmed learning, the integrated day, team teaching, 'Sesame Street' and 'Man: a Course of Study' can all be considered as instructional systems in these terms.

The traditional evaluator builds his study around innovations defined in this way. He examines the blueprint or formalized plan and extracts the project's goals, objectives or desired outcomes. From these, in turn, he derives the tests and attitude inventories he will administer. His aim is to evaluate the instructional system by examining whether, for example, it has 'attained its objectives' or met its 'performance criteria'.

This technological approach fails to recognize the catalogue description for what it is. It ignores the fact that an instructional system, when adopted, undergoes modifications that are rarely trivial. The instructional system may remain as a shared idea, abstract model, slogan or shorthand, but it assumes a different form in every situation. Its constituent elements are emphasized or de-emphasized, expanded or truncated, as teachers, administrators, technicians and students interpret and re-interpret the instructional system for their particular setting. In practice, objectives are commonly re-ordered, re-defined, abandoned or forgotten. The original 'ideal' formulation ceases to be accurate or, indeed, of much relevance. Few in practice take catalogue descriptions and lists of objectives very seriously, save—it seems—for the traditional evaluator. To switch from discussing the instructional system in abstract form to describing the details of its implementation is to cross into another realm. Here the second new concept is required.

The learning milieu

This is the social-psychological and material environment in which students and teachers work together. The learning milieu represents a network or nexus of cultural, social, institutional and psychological variables. These interact in complicated ways to produce, in each class or course, a unique pattern of circumstances, pressures, customs, opinions and work styles which suffuse the teaching and learning that occur there. The configuration of the learning milieu, in any particular classroom, depends on the interplay of numerous different factors. For instance, there are numerous constraints (legal, administrative, occupational, architectural and financial) on the organization of teaching in schools; there are pervasive operating assumptions (about the arrangement of subjects, curricula, teaching methods and student evaluation) held by the staff; there are the individual teacher's characteristics (teaching style, experience, professional orientation and private goals); and there are student perspectives and preoccupations.

Acknowledging the diversity and complexity of learning milieux is an essential pre-requisite for the serious study of educational innovations. The argument advanced here is that innovatory projects, even for research purposes, cannot sensibly be separated from the learning milieux of which they become part. If an evaluation study hinges on the supposed perpetuation of the instructional system in more or less its original form, it makes an arbitrary and artificial distinction: it treats the innovation as a self-contained and independent system, which in practice it is manifestly not.

The introduction of an innovation sets off a chain of repercussions throughout the learning milieu. In turn, these unintended consequences are likely to affect the innovation itself, changing its form and moderating its impact. For example, at the Massachusetts Institute of Technology, it was found that switching from 'distributed' to 'concentrated' study (a change from students taking several subjects concurrently to intensive full-time study of a single subject) was, in the event, far more than a matter of re-timetabling (Parlett and King, 1971). It demanded new pedagogic forms (continuous lecturing would have led to 'overload'); it resulted in new role relationships between staff and students (daily contact encouraged a degree of informality impossible with two meetings a week of one hour each); and it changed peer relations between students (their working alongside the same students continuously led to much greater interaction than is usual in the Institute's sophomore classes). Such profound shifts in the learning milieu produced a further range of important secondary effects, apparently far removed from the innovation as such, but ultimately deriving from it.

To attempt to gauge the impact of the innovation (in this instance concentrated study) without paying attention to factors such as these would clearly be absurd. In the above study it was possible to trace how each of these milieu effects had its corollary in the intellectual sphere: e.g. the informality encouraged normally silent students to ask questions; and though the range of different learning activities was regarded as excellent for achieving basic comprehension of the subject-matter, it might have put the students at a disadvantage in a conventional examination.

Connecting changes in the learning milieu with intellectual experiences of students is one of the chief concerns for illuminative evaluation. Students do not confront 'knowledge' in naked form: it comes to them clothed in texts, lectures, tape-loops, etc. These form part of a wider set of arrangements for instructing, assessing and counselling, which embody core assumptions about how knowledge and pedagogy should be organized. This 'management' framework, in turn, is embedded within wider departmental and institutional structures, each with its own set of procedures, and professional and societal allegiances. Though apparently far removed from the assimilation and schematization of knowledge at the classroom level, these 'higher order' aspects of the school or college environment cannot be ignored. To take an example: teaching and learning in a particular setting are profoundly influenced by the type of assessment procedures in use; by constraints of timetabling; by the size and diversity of classes; by the availability of teaching assistants, library, computing and copying facilities. These, in turn, are dependent on departmental priorities; on policies of faculty promotion; on institutional myths and traditions; and on local and national pressures.

The 'learning milieu' concept is necessary for analysing the interdependence of learning and teaching, and for relating the organization and practices of instruction to the immediate and long-term responses of students. For instance, students' intellectual development cannot be understood in isolation but only within a particular school or college milieu. Equally, there are phenomena of crucial educational significance (such as boredom, interest, concentration, 'floundering', and intellectual dependence) that make nonsense of the traditional psychological distinction between 'cognitive' and 'affective', and which customarily arise as responses to the total learning milieu, not to single components of it. Students do not respond merely to presented content and to tasks assigned. Rather, they adapt to and work within the learning milieu taken as an inter-related whole. They pay close attention to 'hidden' (Snyder, 1971) as well as 'visible' curricula. Besides acquiring particular habits of studying, reading and responding, they also assimilate the conventions, beliefs and models of reality that are constantly and inevitably transmitted through the total teaching process. For studies that examine various aspects of this 'secondary' learning, and its relationship to intellectual development and social context, see Becker, Geer and Hughes (1968), Perry (1968) and Young (1971).

ORGANIZATION AND METHODS OF ILLUMINATIVE EVALUATION

Illuminative evaluations—like the innovations and learning milieux that they study—come in diverse forms. The size, aims and techniques of the evaluation depend on many factors: the sponsors' preoccupations; the exact nature and stage of the innovation; the number of institutions, teachers, and students involved; the level of co-operation and the degree of access to relevant information; the extent of the investigator's previous experience; the time available for data collection; the format of the required report; and, not least, the size of the evaluation budget.

Illuminative evaluation is not a standard methodological package but a general research strategy. It aims to be both adaptable and eclectic. The choice of research tactics follows not from research doctrine, but from decisions in each case as to the best available techniques; the problem defines the methods used, not vice versa. Equally, no method (with its own built-in limitations) is used exclusively or in isolation; different techniques are combined to throw light on a common problem. Besides viewing the problem from a number of angles, this 'triangulation' approach (Webb et al., 1966) also facilitates the cross-checking of otherwise tentative findings.

At the outset, the researcher is concerned to familiarize himself thoroughly with the day-to-day reality of the setting or settings he is studying. In this he is similar to social anthropologists or to natural historians. Like them, he makes no attempt to manipulate, control or eliminate situational variables, but takes as given the complex scene he encounters. His chief task is to unravel it; isolate its significant features; delineate cycles of cause and effect; and comprehend relationships between beliefs and practices, and between organizational patterns and the responses of individuals. Since illuminative evaluation concentrates on examining the innovation as an integral part of the learning milieu, there is a definite emphasis both on observation at the classroom level and on interviewing participating instructors and students.

Characteristically in illuminative evaluation there are three stages: investigators observe, inquire further and then seek to explain. Thus, in our study of a pilot project in independent learning in British secondary schools (Nuffield Resources for Learning Project),* early visits to the participating schools yielded a number of common incidents, recurring trends and issues frequently raised in discussion. These we either observed ourselves or heard

* The background to this is described in Taylor (1971).

about from teachers and pupils. (For example, we noticed that teachers spoke in different ways about the independent learning materials provided for use with their classes. While some regarded the sets of materials as constituting, collectively, a course of study, others saw the same materials as having a supplementary or ancillary function, to be used simply as a collection of resources to draw upon as, when or if necessary).

The second stage began with the selection of a number of such phenomena, occurrences or groups of opinions as topics for more sustained and intensive inquiry. A change of emphasis accompanied this development. During the first, exploratory stage, we had become 'knowledgeable' about the scheme. At the second stage this enabled our questioning to be more focused; communication to be more coherent and relaxed; and, in general, observation and inquiry to be more directed, systematic and selective. (Thus—in our contacts with the teachers—we sought to find out more about the status they assigned to the independent learning materials, and the extent to which they integrated them with others.)

The third stage consisted in seeking general principles underlying the organization of the project; spotting patterns of cause and effect within its operation; and placing individual findings within a broader explanatory context. It began with our weighing alternative interpretations in the light of information obtained. Thus, why did teachers differ in their attitudes towards the materials? It seemed in general that teachers' views depended on the availability of related materials in the school; on their previous experience with similar methods; and, most critically, on whether or not they saw the material as 'displacing' or as 'supporting' the teacher. A number of other lines of investigation led to the same central issue: that of the changed role of the teacher in an independent learning setting.

Obviously the three stages overlap and functionally inter-relate. The transition from stage to stage, as the investigation unfolds, occurs as problem areas become progressively clarified and re-defined. The course of the study cannot be charted in advance. Beginning with an extensive data base, the researchers systematically reduce the breadth of their inquiry to give more concentrated attention to the emerging issues. This 'progressive focusing' permits unique and unpredicted phenomena to be given due weight. It reduces the problem of data overload, and prevents the accumulation of a mass of unanalysed material.

Within this three-stage framework, an information profile is assembled using data collected from four areas: observation, interviews, questionnaires and tests, documentary and background sources.

Observation
As noted above, the observation phase occupies a central place in illuminative evaluation. The investigator builds up a continuous record of ongoing

events, transactions and informal remarks (a useful source of participant observation research methods is McCall and Simmons, 1969). At the same time, he seeks to organize these data at source, adding interpretative comments on both manifest and latent features of the situation. In addition to observing and documenting day-to-day activities of the project, the investigator may also be present at a wide variety of other events (e.g. staff and student meetings, open days, examiners' meetings, etc. For a research study that draws extensively on non-official, 'back of the shop' settings, see Smith and Keith, 1971.)

Much of the on-site observation involves recording discussions with and between participants. These provide additional information which might not otherwise be apparent or forthcoming from more formal interviews. The language conventions, slang, jargon and metaphors that characterize conversation within each learning milieu can reveal tacit assumptions, inter-personal relationships and status differentials.

Finally, there is a place for codified observation, using schedules for recording patterns of attendance, seating, utilization of time and facilities, teacher-pupil interaction, etc. (Nuthall, 1970). The illuminative evaluator is cautious in the deployment of such techniques. In that they record only surface behaviour, they do not facilitate the uncovering of underlying, more meaningful features.

Interviews
Discovering the views of participants is crucial to assessing the impact of an innovation.* Teachers and students are asked about their work, what they think of it, how it compares with previous experiences; and also to comment on the use and value of the innovation. Interviews vary as to the type of information or comment that is sought. While brief structured interviews are convenient for obtaining biographical, historical or factual information, more open-ended and discursive forms are suitable for less straightforward topics (e.g. career ambitions and anxieties).

Though desirable, it is rarely possible to interview every participant except in small projects or with large research teams. Interviewees, therefore, must usually be selected randomly or by 'theoretical' sampling (Glaser and Strauss, 1967). This latter mode requires seeking out informants or particular groups who may have special insight or whose position makes their viewpoints noteworthy (e.g. students who have won prizes or failed altogether; marginal staff members, who may have close knowledge of the innovation but have stayed outside it; young assistants teaching in their first year, etc.). Those interviewed can also include more distant but equally relevant figures: at higher

* Various approaches to interviewing can be found in the social sciences. Contrast the opposing perspectives presented by Hyman et al. (1954) and Cicourel (1964). In that it is more characteristic of the anthropological paradigm, illuminative evaluation favours the latter approach.

education level, heads of department, administrators and student counsellors; and, beyond the college, curriculum developers and foundation officials from whom the innovation stemmed.

Questionnaire and test data
While concentrating on observation and interviews, the illuminative evaluator does not eschew paper-and-pencil techniques. Their advantage in larger scale illuminative studies is especially evident. Also survey-type question-naires, used late in a study, can sustain or qualify earlier tentative findings. Free and fixed response formats can be included to obtain both quantitative summary data and also open-ended (and perhaps new and unexpected) comment. If necessary, these qualitative data can be content-analysed, to furnish further numerical results.

There are, of course, several valid objections to questionnaires, particularly if they are used in isolation. Unless most carefully prepared, questionnaires can lead to mindless accumulations of uninterpretable data. Expensive in time and resources, such careful preparation must be weighed against the benefits likely to accrue. A second drawback is that many recipients regard question-naires as impersonal and intrusive. Others, keen to express their complicated views, find the questionnaire a frustrating, indeed trivializing, medium. From these dissatisfied groups some do not reply, yet these non-respondents may be the most important in certain respects; in an unpublished questionnaire study at Massachusetts Institute of Technology, non-response was found to be the best predictor of student drop-out.

Besides completing questionnaires, participants can also be asked to prepare written comments on the project, to go through checklists, or compile work diaries that record their activities over a specific period of time (Parlett, 1967). Finally, there are published or custom-built tests of attitude, per-sonality and achievement. Such tests enjoy no privileged status within the study. Test scores cannot be considered in isolation; as Stake warns (1973, p. 219);

Educators should continue to be apprehensive about evaluating teaching on the basis of performance testing alone. They should know how difficult it is to represent educational goals with statements of objectives. They should know how costly it is to provide suitable criterion testing. [And] They should know that the common-sense interpretation of these results is frequently wrong . . .

Thus, test scores can form merely one section of the data profile. Interest lies not so much in relating different test scores, but in accounting for them using the study's findings as a whole.

Documentary and background information
Innovations do not arise unheralded. They are preceded by committee minutes, funding proposals, architectural plans and consultants' reports.

C.E.: T.I.—4*

Also, other primary sources are obtainable, e.g. non-confidential data from registrars' offices; autobiographical and eye-witness accounts of the innovation; tape recordings of meetings; and examples of students' assignments. The assembly of such information can serve a useful function. It can provide a historical perspective of how the innovation was regarded by different people before the evaluation began. The data may also indicate areas for inquiry (how representative were the students taking part?); may point to topics for intensive discussion (why were certain major features of the original proposal later abandoned?); or may expose aspects of the innovation that would otherwise be missed (why were subject requirements not fulfilled?). (The above examples are drawn from an illuminative evaluation study of two innovative freshman programmes at Massachusetts Institute of Technology—the Unified Science Study Program and the Experimental Study Group. Each offered a full-time alternative to the traditional first-year programme (Parlett, 1971).)

PROBLEMS AND POSSIBILITIES OF ILLUMINATIVE EVALUATION

First encounters with the radically different perspective of illuminative evaluation prompt a number of important questions.

(*a*) Foremost is usually concern over the 'subjective' nature of the approach. Can 'personal interpretation' be scientific? Is not collection, analysis and reporting of data, sceptics ask, entirely at the discretion of the researchers themselves?

Behind such questions lies a basic but erroneous assumption: that forms of research exist which are immune to prejudice, experimenter bias and human error. This is not so. Any research study requires skilled human judgements and is thus vulnerable (see, for example, Rosenthal, 1966). Even in evaluation studies that handle automatically processed numerical data, judgement is necessary at every stage: in the choice of samples; in the construction or selection of tests; in deciding conditions of administration; in selecting the mode of statistical treatment (e.g. whether or not to use factor analysis); in the relative weight given to different results; and, particularly, in the selection and presentation of findings in reports.

Nevertheless, the extensive use of open-ended techniques, progressive focusing and qualitative data in illuminative evaluation still raises the possibility of gross partiality on the part of the investigator. A number of precautionary tactics are possible. During the investigation, different techniques can be used to cross-check the most important findings; open-ended material can be coded and checked by outside researchers; consultants to the evaluation can be charged with challenging preliminary interpretations and playing devil's advocate; and members of the research team can be commissioned to develop their own interpretations.* At the report stage, in addition to the findings, critical research processes can also be documented: theoretical principles and methodological ground rules can be discussed and made explicit; criteria for selecting or rejecting areas of investigation can be spelled out; and evidence can be presented in such a way that others can judge its quality.

Even with such precautions, the subjective element remains. It is inevitable. When the investigator abandons the agricultural-botany paradigm his role is necessarily re-defined. The use of interpretative human insight and skills is, indeed, encouraged rather than discouraged. The illuminative evaluator thus joins a diverse group of specialists (e.g. psychiatrists, social anthropologists and historians) where this is taken for granted. In each of these fields, the research worker has to weigh and sift a complex array of human evidence and draw conclusions from it.

A further issue also focuses on the position of the investigator. Does not his presence have an effect on the conduct and progress of the innovatory scheme he is studying? Certainly it does; indeed, any form of data collection creates disturbance. Illuminative evaluators recognize this and attempt to be unobtrusive without being secretive; to be supportive without being collusive; and to be non-doctrinaire without appearing unsympathetic.

This leads to an important point: that research workers in this area need not only technical and intellectual capability, but also inter-personal skills. They seek co-operation but cannot demand it. There may be times when they encounter nervousness and even hostility. They are likely to be observing certain individuals at critical times in their lives (e.g. students about to leave, or teachers with a high personal investment in the innovation). The researchers need tact and a sense of responsibility similar to that pertaining in the medical profession. They seek and are given private opinions, often in confidence. They are likely to hear, in the course of their study, a great deal about personalities and institutional politics that others might be inquisitive to know. There are especially difficult decisions to make at the report stage; though full reporting is necessary, it is essential to safeguard individuals' privacy.

Such problems, confronting many research workers in the human sciences, are exacerbated in the case of close-up, intensive studies of the type outlined here. The price of achieving the richer, more informative data of illuminative evaluation is the greatly increased attention that must be paid to the evaluator's professional standards and behaviour. Though there can be no fixed rules, there are certain guidelines for the illuminative evaluator. For instance, to retain the viability and integrity of his research position and the trust of the participants in the project, the investigator needs from the outset to clarify his role, to be open about the aims of his study, and to ensure that there is no

* The added possibility of research 'in tandem', with different investigators working in semi-isolation and pooling their findings at the end, is currently being examined with respect to a proposed British evaluation involving the authors.

misunderstanding or ambiguity about who, for example, will receive the report. He must also not be a 'snooper', nor become an 'institutionalized voyeur' in succumbing to his private research interests. He should also avoid the dangers of 'going native' or getting caught up in political intrigues. (For an early but still relevant discussion of these problems, see various papers in Adams and Preiss, 1960.)

(b) Besides concern with the investigator's special position, illuminative evaluation also prompts questions concerning the scope of the investigation. Is illuminative evaluation confined to small-scale innovations? Can it be applied to innovations that are being widely implemented? Detailed studies of specific learning milieux may be insightful and valid, but are the results and analyses generalizable to other situations? Is it possible to move from the particular to the universal?

Despite its basis in the close-up study of individual learning milieux, illuminative evaluation can also be applied on a wider scale. Suppose a curriculum project had been adopted by many different schools. At the beginning of the evaluation, a small sample of schools could be selected for intensive study. As the study progressed, and as it focused on selected salient issues arising in the different learning milieux, the number of schools studied could be expanded. The new investigations, now more selective, could be pursued more speedily, with the concentration more on noting similarities and differences between situations than on full documentation of each learning milieu. At the same time, it is necessary to remain extremely flexible and to be open to new issues that arise in the later stages of a study. Finally, with this further information assimilated, short visits or even—in the last resort—postal questionnaires could be used for the remainder of the institutions.

The full progression—from small sample studies to larger scale inquiries—is often only necessary in widely applied innovations. But there is another way in which perceptive and rigorous study of specific situations can yield more generally applicable insights with either large-scale or small-scale investigations. Learning milieux, despite their diversity, share many characteristics. Instruction is constrained by similar conventions, subject divisions and degrees of student involvement. Teachers encounter parallel sets of problems. Students' learning, participation, study habits and examination techniques are found to follow common lines; and innovations, as such, face habitual difficulties and provoke familiar reactions. There is a wide range of overlapping social and behavioural phenomena that accompany teaching, learning and innovating. This is widely acknowledged. However, few of these phenomena have been pinpointed, adequately described or defined accurately. Illuminative evaluation aims to contribute to this process. There is a need for abstracted summaries, for shared terminology, and for insightful concepts. These can serve as aids to communication and facilitate theory-building. They have been conspicuously absent from most research in education. Yet, without this conceptual equipment, the universals of teaching will be cyclically discovered, described, forgotten, re-discovered and described again.

DECISION-MAKING, EVALUATION AND ILLUMINATION

The principal purpose of evaluation studies is to contribute to decision-making. However, in practice, motives for commissioning evaluations are often mixed. Some 'evaluations' may be used to delay troublesome decisions or to window-dress a policy already formulated. Exceptionally, they may be instigated simply to satisfy a funding agency's demands.

There are at least three separate but related groups of decision-makers to whom the evaluator addresses his report:

(a) the project's participants;
(b) the project's sponsors, supervisory committee or local education authority;
(c) interested outsiders (such as other researchers, curriculum planners, etc.).

Each group will look to the report for help in making different decisions. The participants, for example, will be anxious to correct deficiencies, make improvements and establish future priorities. The sponsors and the LEA will be concerned with pedagogic issues but will also want to know about the innovation's costs, use of resources and outside reputation. The outsiders will read the report to decide whether or not the scheme has 'worked', or to see whether it could be applied or adapted to their own situations.

Clearly, if the evaluator is to acknowledge the interests of all these groups, he cannot—even if requested—provide a simple 'yes' or 'no' on the innovation's future. A decision based on one group's evaluative criteria would, almost certainly, be disputed by other groups with different priorities. A 'mastery of fundamentals' for one group is for another a 'stifling of creativity'. The investigator does not make decisions. Indeed, in these terms he cannot—except as a representative or agent of one of the interest groups. If the evaluator allows his study to be defined in this way—oriented towards one group only—he accepts the more limited role and quite different tasks of the 'service' researcher.

Illuminative evaluation thus concentrates on the information-gathering rather than the decision-making component of evaluation. The task is to provide a comprehensive understanding of the complex reality (or realities) surrounding the project: in short, to 'illuminate'. In his report, therefore, the evaluator aims to sharpen discussion, disentangle complexities, isolate the significant from the trivial, and raise the level of sophistication of debate.

SUMMARY

When an innovation ceases to be an abstract concept or plan, and becomes part of the teaching and learning in a school or college, it assumes a different form altogether. The theatre provides an analogy: to know whether a play 'works', one has to look not only at the manuscript but also at the performance; that is, at the interpretation of the play by the director and actors. It is this that is registered by the audience and appraised by the critics. Similarly, it is not an instructional system as such, but its translation and enactment by teachers and students, that is of concern to the evaluator and other interested parties. There is no play that is 'director-proof'. Equally, there is no innovation that is 'teacher-proof' or 'student-proof'.

If this is acknowledged, it becomes imperative to study an innovation through the medium of its performance and to adopt a research style and methodology that is appropriate. This involves the investigator leaving his office and computer printout to spend substantial periods in the field. The crucial figures in the working of an innovation—learners and teachers— become his chief preoccupation. The evaluator concentrates on 'process' within the learning milieu, rather than on 'outcomes' derived from a specification of the instructional system. Observation, linked with discussion and background inquiry, enable him to develop an informed account of the innovation in operation. (On the theatre analogy, an agricultural-botany evaluator is rather like a critic who reviews a production on the basis of the script and applause-meter readings, having missed the performance.)

Ideally, the output of his research will be regarded as useful, intelligible and revealing, by those involved in the enterprise itself. Further, by addressing key educational issues, it can also be seen as a recognizable reality by others outside the innovation. If the report is seen merely as an arcane or irrelevant addition to a research literature already ignored by practising educators, clearly the evaluator will have failed.

In attempting to document the teacher-student interactions, intellectual habits, institutional constraints, etc. that characterize classroom life, the investigator contributes to a field that has received only minimal attention from social scientists. This chapter has focused on the evaluation of innovatory projects. However, there is an obvious need (not always acknowledged) for comparable studies to be made of traditional teaching. Illuminative evaluation need not be confined to innovation. Until recently, perceptive accounts of learning milieux have, more often than not, been found in 'travellers' tales' (Holt, 1964) or 'non-fiction' novels (Herndon, 1965) rather than in educational research reports. The investigator has, therefore, not only short-term goals but also the long-term goal of contributing to a developing and urgently required new field of study.

This approach does not cure all ills, nor can any one approach. Certainly, no simplified instant solutions to perennial educational questions will be delivered by such studies. Indeed, by discarding a spurious 'technological' simplification of reality, and by acknowledging the complexity of educational process, the illuminative evaluator is likely to increase rather than lessen the sense of uncertainty in education. On the other hand, unless studies such as these are vigorously pursued, there is little hope of ever moving beyond helpless indecision or doctrinal assertion in the conduct of educational affairs.

6 Some recent evaluation studies of curriculum projects—a review

Michael Eraut

It is suggested that a curriculum development project makes three basic assumptions: (*a*) that its innovation strategy will lead to appropriate implementation in some schools; (*b*) that its curriculum strategy, when followed, will have effects consistent with its intentions; and (*c*) that these effects will have greater educational value than those resulting from alternative strategies. These need to be carefully distinguished and clarified.

Seven evaluation studies of projects are compared for the kinds of information they collected and the techniques they used, and some reasons for the differences are sought. The role of in-service education is emphasized, both within project innovation strategies and as a means of developing teachers' understanding of curriculum innovation as a whole.

INTRODUCTION

In inviting an independent review of recent evaluation studies, my co-authors are clearly determined to practise what they preach. If evaluation is good for projects, then it must be good for evaluators too. But which preacher am I to follow? Am I for example to set up a 'counter-image' to that set up by the evaluators themselves (Kaner, 1973, p. 145)? Am I to be an 'honest broker' and attempt to sell evaluation, warts and all, to those who decide whether to invest in it or not? Or am I to be a 'critical friend' (Sparrow, 1973, p. 2)?

Some evaluators have regretted not being appointed early in the lives of their projects. I was not appointed at all, nor given any resources with which to evaluate the evaluators. Therefore I have had to rely solely on published information, and this constraint has narrowed my choice of role. The published information is mainly about broad strategies, data and conclusions. Restrictions in length have prevented much description of detailed procedures, and the evaluation instruments themselves are seldom available for scrutiny. So I am in no position to assess the technical competence of the evaluators, though I cannot fail to be impressed by the thoroughness with which they tackled their complex tasks. Nor, without additional resources, can I presume to test 'counter-image' hypotheses such as 'evaluation has no effect on the conduct of a project', or 'evaluation evidence has no effect on the adoption of a project'. The first would appear to be disproved by the evaluation studies under review, in spite of the biased source of information; but there is no reported evidence relevant to the second, much more plausible, hypothesis. The 'honest broker' role is also impossible because so much of the interaction between a project team and its evaluator must inevitably be confidential; and the nature and significance of informal unrecorded communication to decision-makers external to the project is also impossible to assess. For similar reasons, I hope that this review will not be given a summative interpretation. My purpose is formative and my role can only be that of a 'critical friend'. My hope is that future evaluators will find the questions I raise both helpful and significant.

The choice of studies for review has again been largely determined by the availability of published information. Six of the seven projects selected had officially designated evaluators and the seventh, Nuffield Advanced Biological Science, shared the evaluation role among team members and outsiders but planned evaluation through a separate evaluation subcommittee (Kelly, 1973a, p. 93). Although the projects themselves (see Table 6.1) are not quite 'first generation', the evaluation studies are the first to have been carried out in formal association with British curriculum development projects. Their pioneering nature is of critical importance in understanding these studies. There was little previous experience to guide the evaluators, and the evaluation strategies as well as the projects needed to be flexible and adaptable to change in the light of further evidence. Not surprisingly, those studies which had sufficient time to alter their strategies and still deliver the relevant information are the more impressive. Information on the timing of the projects and of their formally designated evaluation activities is given in the table.

Before we proceed to consider the evaluations themselves, it is worth

Table 6.1 Projects and evaluation studies under review

Name of project	Funding period of project	Funding period of evaluation
Nuffield Secondary Science	1965–70	1969–70
Nuffield Advanced Biological Science	1965–70	No separate eval.
Humanities Curriculum Project	1967–72	1968–72
Project Technology	1967–72	1969–72
Science 5–13	1967–75	1967–73
Environmental Studies (5–13)	1967–71	1969–71
Programme in Linguistics and English Teaching: Initial Literacy Project	1967–70*	1969–70

* Period of funding by Schools Council.

noting some special features of the projects. Though only three of the evaluation studies were lengthy (4 years or more), five of the seven projects lasted 5 years or more. All the projects except the last two were large and expensive by British standards, and two of them, Science 5–13 and Initial Literacy, built on the foundations of previous projects. This allowed time for revision of materials and strategies, thus making formative evaluation a realistic possibility. Still more atypical of curriculum projects in general is the fact that only two of the seven were 'reforming' projects: Nuffield Advanced Biological Science set out to reform an existing curriculum in an existing slot on the timetable, and Initial Literacy to provide a new approach to the teaching of reading. The Humanities Curriculum Project and Project Technology were what Tawney, Swinswood and Gunn (1973) have called 'initiating' projects, creating new slots or combinations of slots on the timetable; and Science 5–13 and Environmental Studies were also mainly initiatory, affecting both the timing and the location of teaching even when there was no formal timetable. Nuffield Secondary Science was transitional in character, as some schools were already teaching science to pupils of 'average and below average ability', though they often treated it as a very minor activity occupying only two periods a week.

Finally, it should be noted that, whereas all seven projects produced materials for teachers, only four of them—Nuffield Advanced Biological Science, the Humanities Curriculum Project, Initial Literacy and Project Technology—produced materials for pupils. Moreover, only two projects, Nuffield Advanced Biological Science and Project Technology, were involved in developing courses. The biology project concentrated on a single but fairly flexible course, whereas Project Technology only put part of its developmental effort into courses and pupil materials, the rest of it going into teacher materials for more general use. All the other projects left the selection of content and its organization into courses entirely in the hands of the individual school or teacher. Clearly, curriculum development in the United Kingdom is much more teacher-based in its products and in its intentions than is curriculum development in most other countries (Maclure, 1968), where the main emphasis is on pupil materials and course development. This difference is reflected in the way evidence from teachers dominates all other forms of evidence in the evaluation studies under review. But have we, in the United Kingdom, over-reacted to this special characteristic of our projects? Or have we failed to make sufficient allowance for it in devising our own evaluation strategies? My answer, paradoxically, is a bit of both. So let us examine the evidence.

THE AIMS OF THE EVALUATION STUDIES

As mentioned above, few British projects have been concerned with producing completely prescribed curricula. The term 'curriculum strategy' is perhaps

more appropriate, conveying as it does the idea of a set of inter-related significant decisions. Even when the support materials give quite detailed advice,
the tactical decisions are invariably left to the teacher (and often many of the
strategic ones too!). Nor have the projects confined their activities to designing or developing curriculum strategies. They have also been concerned with
persuading and assisting teachers to adopt these curriculum strategies; and
for this purpose each project has had an 'innovation strategy', though it has
often been implicit rather than explicit. In project terms, Cooper's emphasis
(Chapter 1, p. 6) on information about feasibility, effectiveness, and educational value can be seen in terms of three main assumptions:

(a) that the project's innovation strategy will lead to a significant number
    of schools implementing the curriculum strategy as intended (not just
    adopting the project's name and materials);
(b) that the project's curriculum strategy, if correctly implemented, will
    have effects on the pupil, teacher and school which are consistent with
    the project's claims and intentions;
(c) that these effects will have greater educational value than the effects of
    possible alternative strategies.

All the projects under review have made these assumptions, which have not
always been explicitly stated. Consequently, evaluators have often failed to
differentiate between them. There is little evidence that they have distinguished a project's value judgements from its empirical judgements, or seen
fit to elucidate the arguments for and against its curriculum strategy. Instead,
evidence relevant to the second assumption seems to have been implicitly
used to justify the third. Many studies have also conflated the first two assumptions, with the result that they have looked for effects in 'project' schools
without knowing whether the schools had followed or even understood the
project's advice. When trial schools are still getting used to a project's ideas,
and their curricula vary greatly in their congruency with the project's curriculum strategy, it is hardly reasonable to expect any measurement of outcomes
to be a fair indication of the effectiveness of that strategy. A useful summative
evaluation of the project's curriculum strategy is impossible until its innovation strategy has been at least partially successful. Only formative evaluation
is feasible in the early stages of a project, and public demand for preliminary
summative information has to be treated with extreme tact.

What, then, are the possible aims of the formative component of a project's
evaluation activities ? In terms of the project alone, the aim can be to provide
information relevant to the 'improvement' of either its innovation strategy
or its curriculum strategy or both. Usually the innovation strategy will
include several elements: conferences and courses; advisory committees;
team visits to schools; teacher materials; project publications; articles in
national journals and newspapers; and local support in the form of meetings,

visits, courses, etc. Most of these activities are controlled by the project and nearly all could benefit from formative evaluation. Then we also have to take into account the fact that members of the project team are not the only decision-makers who are likely to benefit from formative evaluation. Nor, indeed, are they the only people to have an innovation strategy. Each LEA and school involved will have its own innovation strategy, though it will probably be implicit and it may not even be congruent with that of the project. Individual teachers also are likely to have personal innovation strategies as they seek to gain various kinds of support from their school or LEA. Appropriate information could help all three of these groups—teachers, schools and LEAs—to 'improve' their strategies, and hence indirectly to validate the first assumption by ensuring that a significant number of schools implement the project's curriculum strategy.

The curriculum strategy can also be considered in terms of several elements, always very closely inter-related. It may include decisions about content, teaching style, pupil activities, intended outcomes and even assessment, as well as more detailed support in the form of teacher materials or pupil materials. Indeed, one of the most critical features of formative evaluation not usually reported is the extent to which the main curriculum decisions of the project are still open to alteration in the light of feedback, as distinct from their more detailed elaboration. We shall return to this question later when we discuss the pilot phase. Meanwhile, it should be noted that even the project's more detailed elaboration of its curriculum strategy will be subject to much further amplification and possibly also some alteration, as each separate teacher or group of teachers prepares to implement it. In a very real sense, each teacher will have his own personal version of the curriculum and appropriate feedback could help him to improve it. The evaluator has a double role here: assisting teachers in their own personal formative evaluation, an activity which ought to be fairly closely linked with their feedback to the project; and then sharing with teachers in a digestible form the relevant aspects of the project's own information collection. Such assistance might increase the effectiveness of the project's curriculum strategy, and would also increase the likelihood of the teachers concerned contributing on future occasions either to the project itself or to their own local colleagues.

A list of possible aims for formative evaluation has been drawn up in Table 6.2, which shows how the seven projects selected their formative evaluation priorities. Some possible explanation for the differences between projects will be offered later on. Meanwhile, it is worth noting that the main emphasis in the evaluation studies under review was on providing formative information relevant to the project's curriculum strategy. Much less attention was given to the project's innovation strategy, especially to the improvement of in-service courses and the development of local support. It could also be argued that more notice should have been taken of the needs of decision-

Table 6.2 Selection by seven projects of priorities for formative evaluation

Information about	Nuffield Sec. Science	Nuffield Adv. Biol. Science	Humanities Curriculum	Project Technology	Science 5–13	Environmental Studies	Initial Literacy
Innovation strategies							
Conferences and courses			I		I		
Team visits							
Project publications				F			
Articles							
Teacher materials*					F		F
Local support systems			F				
Curriculum strategies							
Content	F	F			F		F
Teaching style	F		F		F		F
Pupil activities	F	F	F		F		F
Intended outcomes	X	F	X	F	F	X	F
Assessment/diagnosis		F	X	F	F	X	F
Course materials		F	I	F	F		F

Key: F—formally reported in documents or meetings;
    I—Informally reported in casual discussion (coverage unknown and possibly not very great);
    X—not relevant.

* This refers to materials explaining the project's strategy and philosophy, and does not include course materials.

making groups other than the project itself. This might have helped counteract some of the inherent problems of innovations based on central development and subsequent dissemination (Eraut, 1972). Project, LEA, school and teacher cannot be co-partners in innovation if the distribution of information between them is too uneven.

When one moves to the summative component of a project's evaluation activities, the range of aims is wider still because there are more decision-makers and more divergent needs for information. But most groups of decision-makers will want evidence on the validity of the second assumption —that the project's curriculum strategy, if correctly implemented, will have effects on the pupil, teacher and school which are consistent with the project's claims and intentions—and also on unintended outcomes. Few, however, will realize the improbability of reaching simple conclusions of a definitive nature. Parlett and Hamilton (Chapter 5, pp. 86–8) have already emphasized the complexity of educational situations and shown how simple conclusions are likely to be either impossible or else dangerously misleading. But this does not release the evaluator from the obligation to provide decision-makers with relevant evidence, e.g. 'These tests did not indicate any differences but most of the teachers thought the pupils had shown much more initiative than in previous years'. The studies under review have also shown the need for the evaluator to anticipate the importance of evidence that is relatively context specific, e.g. 'This is what happened in School A and this is what happened in School B. The reasons for the difference seem to be . . .' or 'The evidence suggests a close link between these particular context characteristics and this particular outcome.'

Another point, made by Parlett and Hamilton and supported by Harlen (Chapter 3, pp. 30–1), is the small range of effects with which the so-called 'classical' evaluation studies were concerned. Such studies rarely shifted their attention from the single dimension of pupil achievement. Most of the studies under review went well beyond this although some, perhaps wrongly, neglected it. The favourite additional dimensions were those of attitudinal change and the development of transferable cognitive skills such as problem-solving. Both present enormous technical difficulties, which some of the studies have reported in detail and others have virtually ignored, but it would take a separate chapter to examine these particular problems. However, in spite of the discouraging experience of the evaluators in this group of studies, we cannot afford to ignore this area of investigation because it is precisely along these dimensions that the greatest claims for new curricula are so frequently made. Only the Humanities Curriculum Project assessed aspects of the personal development of pupils, though other reports mentioned it incidentally. One might have expected more definite attempts to provide information on the development of skills like working independently, contributing productively to task groups or discussion groups, and communicating knowledge and ideas to other people. Then, perhaps most important of all in the eyes of parents, and indeed of many pupils, are the effects of curriculum change on pupils' formal examination results and on their career interests and prospects. One wonders, for example, whether the implementation of Science 5–13 or Environmental Studies in middle or secondary schools has affected the choice of subjects at ages thirteen, fifteen or even sixteen; and whether association with Project Technology has increased the proportion of pupils seeking technological careers.

When we move from effects on pupils to consider effects on teachers and on schools, we are no longer purely concerned with the project's curriculum strategy. Many of the effects may stem from its innovation strategy or, more probably, from some combination of the two. On the positive side we may look for signs of teachers developing new attitudes and skills, and on the negative side for disillusion or avoidance. Innovations can bring both increased enthusiasm and increased work. Does the enthusiasm increase or decrease with time? Does the extra preparation time when the project is first introduced fall to more normal proportions as the teacher gains in experience? How have 'project' teachers affected their colleagues? Has their other work suffered through lack of time, or gained through increased morale and teacher development? And what are the effects on the school as a whole: disruptive or creative tension, a draining of resources from other areas of the curriculum or a stimulus to further innovation? Much of this information will be context specific but many decision-makers will want to have it.

Table 6.3 shows how the projects under review chose to provide information about the effects of adoption. It also indicates whether these effects were related to pupil characteristics, variations in the school's curriculum strategy and variations in the school's context. Finally, it indicates whether or not the evaluator made a clear distinction between the effects of the project being 'correctly' implemented, and the effects of the project in situations where the adopted curriculum strategy was not congruent with project's intentions. Only two of the seven studies fulfilled this important criterion. A lot of the other gaps in this table can be attributed to lack of resources, but some of them, it might be argued, have resulted from an inappropriate evaluation strategy. These points will be developed later when the studies are considered individually.

Information of potential use to decision-makers is not confined to information about the effects of adoption. It we take the first assumption, that the project's innovation strategy is effective, and modify it to suit the dissemination stage by shifting the emphasis to the innovation strategies of LEAs and schools, several questions arise. What has been the relationship between various LEA strategies, school strategies and successful or unsuccessful implementation? What forms of in-service course have been most effective? What support does a teacher need from his school and LEA when he first starts to use the project's curriculum strategy? What continuing support does he need? How, if at all, can the innovation be used to catalyse other innovations? How can the implementation of a project survive when the original teacher leaves? How can the project be best explained to parents? The Humanities Curriculum Project paid considerable attention to these problems, and so did Nuffield Advanced Biological Science (though mainly in a separate research study after the formal conclusion of the project); but the other evaluation studies virtually ignored them (Science 5–13 did a late survey, which was reported to the LEAs concerned). All seven studies, however, have documented the need for in-service support; and many found that it was not being adequately met.

Finally we come to the third assumption, which concerns the educational value of the projects. Many decision-makers would like to know about possible alternative approaches and the arguments for and against each of them. None of the evaluation studies saw fit to provide this kind of information.

Was it because the evaluators were too committed to their projects? Some feasibility arguments against their projects were reported by the Humanities

Table 6.3   Provision of information by seven projects on the effects of project adoption

	Nuffield Sec. Science	Nuffield Adv. Biol. Science	Humanities Curriculum	Project Technology	Science 5–13	Environmental Studies	Initial Literacy
Effects on pupils							
Achievement		√		√	√	√	√
Motivation		√					√
Attitude change	√		√	√	√		
General cognitive development		√	√	√	√	√	
Personality			√				
Working skills*		√					
Exam. results		√			×	×	×
Subject choice	√						×
Careers		√					×
Effects on teachers							
Attitudes		√	√	√	√	√	√
Work demand		√					√
Skill development			√				
Effects on parents	√						
Effects on schools							
Timetable	√		√				
Resource demand		√					
Innovation climate			√				
Effects related to pupil characteristics		√					
Effects related to school curriculum strategy	√		√		√		√
Effects related to context variables		√	√	√	√		√
Distinction between effects of 'correct' and 'incorrect' implementation			√				√

Key: √ —investigated; ×—not relevant.

* Working independently, working in groups, communication skills, etc.

Curriculum Project and Environmental Studies. But no value arguments were reported against any project, not even in the form of press cuttings. Nor was there any reference to alternative approaches. It could, of course, be argued that this should be left to individual advisers, lecturers, wardens and teachers, but shouldn't they receive some support from the 'big battalions'? It is not impossible to provide an analysis of this sort which does not pre-empt the final judgement. One could even add to it by collecting the opinions of mature and respected educators.

THE TECHNIQUES USED

Steadman has already discussed the range of possible techniques (Chapter 4, pp. 57–78), and Table 6.4 indicates which techniques were actually used in the evaluation studies under review. The general pattern confirms a number of features already commented on. The major source of information was provided by the teachers themselves, partly because it was the easiest, partly because most of the publications were aimed at teachers, and partly because most of the studies emphasized formative rather than summative information. However, much of this information appears to have been gathered either at a distance or in structured interviews; and in the author's experience this is insufficient contact to release teachers from their self-imposed obligation to 'say something nice'. It takes much longer to establish the kind of *rapport* which makes honest comment possible; and few will feel free to make radical criticisms rather than suggestions for minor alterations. Teacher meetings can give more chance for criticisms to develop if they are appropriately handled; and they are also more likely to lead to constructive improvements. This kind of feedback is particularly important in the early stages of a project.

Similar arguments could be made about collecting information from pupils. But pupils seem to have been regarded more as guinea-pigs for testing than as people who might make useful contributions. Has the large number of trial schools made the experiences of the individual pupil seem too insignificant? Often, it is the project's dissemination strategy rather than its evaluation strategy which determines the number of trial schools; and the word 'trial' is a confusing misnomer. Several of the studies suggest that the scale of the trials was over-ambitious, with a resultant drop in the quality of support which the project could offer. In this situation the likelihood of the curriculum strategies on trial being congruent with that of the project itself is sharply reduced, as also is the likelihood of the evaluator being able to collect evidence in depth. This issue of scale versus scope is more fully discussed by Harlen (Chapter 3, pp. 48–50). The model with which she concludes her chapter is an excellent compromise, which also makes the crucial distinction between evaluation of the project's curriculum strategy and evaluation of its innovation strategy (pp. 52–3).

Table 6.4 Techniques used by seven evaluation studies

	Nuffield Sec. Science	Nuffield-Adv. Biol. Science	Humanities Curriculum	Project Technology	Science 5-13	Environmental Studies	Initial Literacy
Information from pupils							
Reviews of pupil work	√			√			√
Interviews with pupils	√	√			√		√
Pupil questionnaires	√						
Achievement tests	√			√	√	√	√
Transfer tests	√			√	√		
Attitude tests	√	√		√	√		
Personality tests			√				
Exam. performance	√						
Information from teachers							
Teacher diaries	√			√	√		
Assessment of pupils	√			√	√		
Interviews with teachers	√		√	√	√	√	√
Meetings with teachers	√		√				
Teacher questionnaires	√	√	√	√	√		√
Attitude tests	√				√	√	
Teacher reviews of materials	√			√	√		√
Case studies			√			*	
Information from visitors							
Reports of visits	√				√	√	√
Observation schedules	√						
Case studies of schools			√			*	
Other information							
Case studies of LEAs			√				
Reviews by 'experts'	√						

* Published as a project book but not part of the evaluation study.

SOME COMMENTS ON SPECIFIC STUDIES

Hitherto, the seven studies have been taken as a single group, and attention has focused on common emphases and omissions. The comparative tables do, however, show marked differences between the studies, both in their aims and in their techniques. Some possible reasons for this divergence are listed below:

(a) *the nature of the project:* its innovation strategy, its curriculum strategy, the subject area, the degree of novelty, the magnitude of the 'innovation barrier' and its links with the 'outside world';

(b) *the timing:* of trials, of draft and final publications, and of the evaluation study itself;

(c) *the resources available:* within the evaluation team itself, within the project team, and in the form of outside support, e.g. committee members, reviewers, and local organizers and observers;

(d) *attitudes:* of team members, committee members, teachers, heads, advisers, etc.;

(e) *different value judgements:* on goal priorities for the evaluation;

(f) *different empirical judgements:* as to the most appropriate techniques for a given goal;

(g) *the knowledge, skills and predispositions* of the evaluators themselves.

Some of these influences will be further explored in the comments which follow; and the opportunity will also be taken to point out features of special interest in specific studies.

Nuffield Advanced Biological Science (Kelly, 1971b; 1972a–d; 1973a)

This project probably had more initial factors in its favour than any of the others. At the time it began, the Nuffield Foundation's programme for reforming science curricula was well under way, and procedures and expectations were established. It was aiming to reform a clearly defined section of the curriculum, sixth form biology; and it was the logical successor to Nuffield (O level) Biology. It could also be seen as an agency acting in co-operation with two important reference groups, the Association for Science Education and the Institute of Biology. This eased the problem of finding interested outsiders who could fulfil the roles of committee members, expert reviewers, trial teachers and regional organizers. In addition to this, by fitting naturally into the examination structure, the project had a built-in summative evaluation component and could concentrate on developing an examination which was congruent with its objectives. In spite of being the first of the Nuffield science projects to have a clear evaluation strategy, it made very good use of its advantages from the outset.

Its pilot phase, reported by Kelly (1973a) and cited by Tawney (Chapter 2, p. 16), adopted a model which most other evaluators would envy for its flexibility and breadth of consultation. This led to agreement on nine student objectives and sixteen course objectives. These latter were subdivided into intentions regarding content, approach and feasibility, and used as guidelines for intrinsic evaluation of the course by teachers and experts. Then the examination was used both as a summative check against the accusation of lowering standards and as formative evidence on the achievment of objectives. Additional formative evidence was obtained from teachers, pupils and visitors, but there was no attempt at any systematic observation of teaching, which might have been inconsistent with the kind of relationship the project had with its trial schools. Important points, such as the tendency to over-emphasize the role of practical work in a 'discovery' approach at the sixth form level and to misunderstand the problem of mathematical competence, were picked up and investigated further. As a result of the evidence, radical changes were made in the organization of the course content; the objectives were clarified, and even in one or two cases abandoned.

This study, together with the first phase of Science 5–13, was the closest of the seven to the 'classical' Tyler model, which is elaborated and criticized in Chapter 3. But its objectives were more flexible and formulated at a more general level, and it was much richer in its use of different sources of evidence for formative evaluation. It concentrated almost entirely on the project's curriculum strategy; and for this purpose the model clearly served it well. But it could be argued that a preoccupation with the model diverted attention from a critical evaluation of its innovation strategy. The subsequent creation of a research project on dissemination is presumably a recognition of this problem.

Science 5–13 (Harlen, 1973; 1975)

This was the only project of the seven to have a single person designated as an evaluator from the beginning. She was preparing draft tests and question-naires while materials were still at a very early pilot stage, and her comments on this are worth quoting (Harlen, 1975, p. 15):

... it was felt beneficial—even if uncomfortable—to have someone in the team who had to ask needling questions. To prepare test items for children or ques-tionnaire items for teachers meant probing the material thoroughly, digging down to find what children were intended to achieve from the activities, and how teachers were expected to guide their children. During the development of evaluation material, writers could not avoid facing these crucial questions, nor could the evaluator avoid coming to grips with the essential purpose of the material. One result was a greater awareness on the part of both writers and evaluator of the others' problems and a sharpening of thought among all team members about the task they were jointly undertaking.

A further distinctive feature of this project was the evaluator's role in clarifying the rationale and assisting in writing the general teachers' guide, *With Objectives in Mind*. The guide provided a rationale for the child-centred methods advocated and suggested objectives which were appropriate in terms of children's development. By cross-referencing with these objectives, each of the separate units was able to link pupil activities which were primarily content-focused with possible outcomes which were essentially process-focused. This provided teachers with many useful suggestions for activities and a framework to ensure progression, without pre-empting their freedom to select learning activities according to the needs and interests of individual children and the opportunities of the moment. In addition, an attempt to support teacher diagnosis of pupils' development with 'diagnostic statements' was piloted towards the end of the project, and is now being further developed in a new research project, Progress in Learning Science.

Many of the above features of the project can be attributed to the role of the evaluator as a special kind of team member, sharpening its strategies during the pilot phase and guiding their subsequent revision. In the trials phase, however, this particular evaluator concentrated almost entirely on the formative aim of supplying her colleagues with evidence relevant to revising the project materials for publication. This is well documented, and so is her own formative self-evaluation as she altered her strategy to improve the flow of information and reduce the cost of obtaining it. Of special significance is her abandonment of pupil testing and her classical evaluation model because of its high cost and low information content for formative purposes; her elegant use of cluster analysis to characterize different types of trial schools so she could let her colleagues know from what kind of context each critical comment came; and the development of a teacher's Preferences Form (Harlen, 1975, p. 52) to identify the kinds of methods and activities that each teacher preferred.

To have done more would have required more resources, but it is worth noting the need for more information in addition to the longitudinal sum-mative evaluation of pupil development which the evaluator herself identified. How much science was being taught in the trial schools, and how did adoption of the project affect the balance of the curriculum as a whole? Were the revised units any more acceptable to the less progressive teachers and did they lead to any changes in teaching style? Did the successful teachers feel they had developed their skills as a result of the project, and if so did it transfer to other areas of the curriculum? What were the effects of different innovation strategies in different areas and on different types of teachers?

Humanities Curriculum Project (MacDonald, 1973; Hamingson, 1973)
This study was also a substantial one, involving as many as four evaluators in its final phase. The first evaluator, however, still missed the pilot phase by being appointed a year late. In almost every respect he adopted the opposite strategy to Science 5–13, and the result is equally fascinating. Whereas Science 5–13 could rely on a fair number of teachers already using the pro-ject's recommended teaching style, the Humanities Curriculum Project was trying to develop an entirely new one. It possessed 'many of the hallmarks of past innovation failures. It required induction courses for teachers; it was difficult to use; it was costly in terms of school resources; it conflicted with established values' (MacDonald, 1973, p. 81). So it was not surprising that there was little uniformity of approach in the trial schools and much mis-understanding of the project's ideas. Hence evaluation of the project's curri-

culum strategy was quite impossible at this stage. Instead, the evaluator explored problems of implementation, an essential feature of the project's innovation strategy.

Both the complexity of an innovation of this type, in which practically every LEA, school and teacher had a different strategy, and the evaluator's desire to understand and interpret what was going on rather than give just a superficial description led to a heavy reliance on case studies. 8 case studies of schools and 4 case studies of LEAs were finally completed, and teacher questionnaires from a larger sample of 100 schools were also used. The strong emphasis on the study of innovation strategies was peculiar to this project; and it even included an evaluation of the training courses, which the other evaluators regrettably ignored.

Summative evidence of the curriculum strategy was of a rather unusual kind, including both an extensive psychometric testing programme and a collect of 'judgements' by teachers and pupils. The testing programme used four categories of schools—experienced, trained, untrained and control—but did not include any observational data to indicate how closely any of them approximated to the project's curriculum strategy. They did include the case study schools, however, so some links may be established at an unknown future date. Several of the tests showed gains in trained or experienced schools but not in untrained or control schools, thus providing yet further evidence for the importance of the project's innovation strategy. It is interesting to note that, apart from three tests on vocabulary, reading comprehension and abstract thinking, all the tests related to what this author suspects was the project's real aim, the reduction of alienation, and none of them to the project's expressed aim, 'to develop an understanding of social situations and human acts and of the controversial value issues which they raise' (MacDonald, 1973, p. 82). This aim is expanded in a section of *The Humanities Project: an Introduction* (Schools Council/Nuffield Foundation, 1970) entitled 'Judgement of students' work', which offers ten criteria, e.g. 'To what extent can the student . . . recognise and deal with ambiguity in evidence?' (p. 35). But these criteria appear to have been ignored by the evaluator. Interesting also is the inclusion in *Towards Judgement* (Hamingson, 1973) of an article by a team member on 'The nature of "understanding" ', which in a different project might have resulted from an evaluator trying to clarify the project's rationale during its pilot phase. What emerges from the various evaluation reports, however, is a strong 'feel' for the project in action; and a convincing demonstration of the need for in-service education and the careful planning and monitoring of innovation strategies. The days of simple evaluation studies are over!

Project Technology (Tawney, Swinswood and Gunn, 1973; Tawney et al., 1973; Tawney, 1973; Dennien et al., 1973)

This evaluation study occupied the last three years of a five-year project and was conducted from a separate site. The emphasis is primarily formative; and, since both the timing and the separation made it unlikely that the evaluators would influence the project's overall strategy, they were advised to concentrate on the improvement of the teaching materials. This considerable task was tackled by a series of small-scale studies, designed to cover a reasonable proportion of the project's diverse set of publications, and a single, more comprehensive study of a CSE course in Control Technology. In the smaller studies the main technique used was the teacher questionnaire, and in about half of them this was supplemented by interviews using checklists. A major limitation was the fact that most of the materials were concerned almost entirely with content and offered little guidance on objectives or pedagogy. Apart from a strong commitment to project work, Project Technology did not have a clear curriculum strategy in the same sense as the other projects under review. To have documented the various strategies used in the trial schools would have required an expensive series of case studies and provided relatively little feedback for the revision of materials. Moreover, in technology more than in almost any other subject, the problems of getting things to work prevent teachers from thinking about objectives or teaching strategies until they have had one or two years' experience. So the case studies would merely have recorded a transitional phase.

The smaller studies indicated an important need for in-service training and for more guidance on objectives and pedagogy; and similar conclusions came from the longer study of the CSE course in Control Technology (Tawney et al., 1973). Here, an analysis of several Mode III submissions and examinations indicated considerable departures from the objectives of the original course, which were apparently not recognized as such. The study also used structured and unstructured observation, and tested the achievement of some of the course objectives. This testing proved extremely difficult outside the area of simple comprehension and application. An attitude test had to be abandoned; and the evaluators did eventually develop a reliable test of some important aspects of technological problem-solving but, as so often is the case, its validity was doubtful.

The substantial investment of the project in materials and publications may have forced the evaluators' hand, but it is difficult to see why no attention was paid to the factors influencing the presence or absence of technology in schools. If one overarching aim stands out in the project's publicity, it is that of getting more technology into schools, and there is no evidence on the appropriateness for this purpose of the project's strategy, irrespective of the quality of the materials. In this connexion some investigation of local support systems and in-service training courses might also have been useful, and it is regrettable that the Schools Council was unable to fund a proposal to investigate this area. The evaluators did, however, study the effects of the project's periodicals and confirmed their usefulness for the existing readership. But was the readership sufficient for implementation of the project's aims?

Environmental Studies (Crossland and Moore, 1974)
This two-year study had three components: a study of outcomes, a study of 'contributing factors' and a study of acceptability. The first of these was rather unsatisfactory, as the evaluators themselves acknowledge; and it shows all the symptoms of an evaluator in a hurry. Two instruments were used, the study skills component of the Bristol Achievement Tests and a specially developed map test. Although these were chosen as a result of discussions with the project team, one doubts if they would have been selected if the evaluators had had more time for an intrinsic evaluation of the project materials (see later), or a study of the work in the phase 1 schools, as a basis for inferring likely outcomes. Inadequate resources may have forced this decision, but not many proponents of the environmental studies approach would regard paper-and-pencil tests alone as a valid indication of many of their intended outcomes, particularly those concerned with the processes of information acquisition rather than their product. Instead, the desire to find something conveniently measurable appears to have resulted in the testing of skills that were not specially characteristic of the environmental approach. This suggests that the second of the evaluators' questions, 'Do "standards" suffer as a result of using the EVS approach?' might have been more easily answered than the first, 'Does children's learning improve as a result of using the approach?' (1974, p. 8) But then the full battery of Bristol Achievement Tests would have been more appropriate. Significant improvements on either test could have been attributed to the teacher spending more time on the topic concerned, presumably at the expense of something else. As it is, there is no record of how much time teachers spent on map work nor even of whether they actually used the project's publication, *Starting from Maps*. Another problem is the fact that only half of the experimental group was considered to be using the project's curriculum strategy in a valid manner, and even they could hardly have got used to it in view of the long time required for full understanding and implementation of the project's suggestions (1974, p. 26).

The other two components of the evaluation have more significance for the decision-maker. The first involved fairly lengthy interviews by team members using a checklist. They visited schools at the end of the trial period, but were asked to make use of information gathered on previous visits as well. This showed that just over half the teachers were using a 'valid' EVS approach, and about half were properly aware of skill development—an essential aspect of the project's curriculum strategy. More encouraging was the fact that both the validity of the work and the extent of adoption of the EVS approach were increasing. Proper implementation was shown to relate mainly to teacher variables—female, under forty, primary trained, teaching younger children, favourable to informal methods. The only school or locality factor of importance was access to some personal advisory source.

The study of acceptability used loosely structured interviews with teachers to try and elicit the main arguments for and against the project. This information is invaluable for anyone planning a dissemination strategy, and would have been useful for formative evaluation of the *Teachers' Guide* if it had been done earlier. Obviously the evaluators had to limit their work, but with this project the innovation strategy was particularly critical. Thus, the gathering of formative evidence for revising the *Teachers' Guide* and a study of the in-service training and support system might have been included. One also feels that this project would have greatly benefited from an earlier appointment of the evaluator, which would have allowed interaction between team and evaluator in its pilot stages. The project's curriculum strategy might have been further clarified, and the evaluator might have had time to appreciate the aims of the project earlier.

Nuffield Secondary Science (Alexander, 1973; 1974)
This evaluation was necessarily the most limited of the seven, as it lasted only a year and had a part-time evaluator. The project itself produced teacher materials on eight themes from which teachers were expected to construct their own courses. It emphasized experimental work and pupil involvement, and the main criterion for content selection was that the work should have *significance* for pupils. The evaluator therefore decided to concentrate on the concept of significance, the involvement of pupils and possible changes in attitudes towards science. A questionnaire designed to assess the project's impact on schools looked at the numbers of students involved in the fourth and fifth years, the effects of differing CSE policies and the attitudes of parents and non-project teachers, both science and non-science. Attitudes were on the whole very favourable, but it also emerged that a dominant aspect of 'significance' was not only the teachers' but also the pupils' perception of CSE needs. However, when teachers were asked to explain their choice of routes through the course, only '17% quoted reasons which clearly indicated that the relevance to the pupils' interest was dominant' (1974, p. 8). Unfortunately, there were no resources to pursue the theme of significance any further. It might have been a fascinating study.

The National Foundation for Educational Research's *Pupil Opinion Poll: Science* (no. 104) was used with a control group and pre- and post-testing. Although the attitude towards science teachers improved in the trial schools, most of the other attitudes deteriorated in both groups. This is apparently

C.E.: T.I.—5

normal, and it may of course be due to factors quite unrelated to the science curriculum (see Tawney in Chapter 2, p. 21).

The most interesting part of this study was the approach to pupil involvement. This was based on a simple observation schedule and a 'volunteer' visitor for each of ten schools. He was usually a local science education lecturer or adviser, and he completed nine or ten observations of sample lessons during the course of a year. Twelve categories of activity were used, and recording took place in consecutive five-minute periods throughout the lesson. The schedule seems to have been easy to use and reliable; and one regrets that some of the other evaluation studies did not try something similar. An important finding was that the teaching style moved towards increased pupil participation during the course of the year, though not to a totally 'open-ended' approach. These schools were new to the project and it would have been interesting to have had comparative data on schools which had been using the project materials for longer, as well as some clearer indication from members of the project themselves as to how 'open-ended' they expected the inquiry to be. In this connexion a study of the design, use and effects of worksheets would have been useful; and one gets the impression that this might have been the evaluator's next move if time and resources had allowed.

Initial Literacy (Reid, 1975)

This one-year study took place in the second year of trials, but was too late to be of any value in revising the draft materials for publication. However, it is useful to think of it as having a formative as well as a summative purpose because it provides formative information to teachers, schools and advisers who need to improve implementation and in-service support. Strategically it is a marvellous example of an evaluator with limited resources ignoring all the conventional demands for *scale* and concentrating on *scope*. As a result, we get a clearer picture of 'how it is' than in any of the other studies.

Interviews with children were used to find out about their use of the folders and their linguistic understanding; and seven schools were visited to assess pupil motivation, teaching style, the effects of organizational variables such as vertical grouping, and the use of the sentence maker and word maker in the *Breakthrough to Literacy* materials. Then opinions were collected from eighty-one teachers by an open-ended questionnaire which only asked for 'advantages', 'disadvantages' and 'additional comments'; and this was followed up by interviews with a smaller sample of teachers. These separate sources of evidence combined to give a picture of the scheme in use, and indicated where the project's curriculum strategy had been least understood. These 'problem areas' were also confirmed by a particularly valuable analysis of children's work, which showed how it developed with age, and related mistakes to linguistic misunderstandings.

Teacher judgements on progress were collected by a second questionnaire, which asked about the ability of individual children to read the project booklets and use the sentence maker and word maker. Though the project was at least as much concerned with writing as with reading, it was also felt important to gather some summative evidence on reading performance using criteria external to the project. Three groups of three schools were tested: a first experimental group using the scheme as intended; a second experimental group following the project's intentions not quite so closely; and a control group. All three groups were matched for socio-economic level and environmental conditions, but the control group turned out to have a median age six months higher. The *Neale Analysis* test was used for the top 58 per cent, and indicated a superiority of six months or more for the first experimental group in speed, accuracy and comprehension. Since the Neale test could not be used below a certain level (58 per cent for the control group but 80 per cent for the experimental group), a paragraph reading test based on the *Breakthrough* 'core' vocabulary was used on the bottom 55 per cent. This time both experimental groups out-performed the control group in spite of the age disadvantage. Though not statistically valid, this was encouraging evidence which indicated the potential of the approach.

In summary, the study makes it quite clear what is involved in adopting *Breakthrough* and provides a superb brief for in-service training courses. One's only regret is that it came too late to affect any of the project's publications.

FOUR FINAL ISSUES

Unreported evidence
With the exception of Nuffield Advanced Biological Science, all the studies under review were separately funded evaluations (while the evaluation of Science 5–13 was not separately funded, it did have an officially designated evaluator). The discussion has therefore been confined to the activities of the evaluators. Though interviews and visits by team members have been included when they came under the general direction of the evaluator, most of the evaluation activities of team members were not reported and have therefore been excluded. This is unfortunate, because much of the work done by an evaluator on one project was done by team members on another. (Not appointing an evaluator does not necessarily save money!) What we cannot tell is whether this mattered. No evaluator is free publicly to record who influenced whom, and whether or not project members were receptive to evidence of the need for changes in their strategies; and why should we believe the evaluator anyway? An inside study of a project's pilot phase would require a properly trained field worker who documented changing perceptions and events as they happened. Without this evidence it would be impossible to avoid retrospective rationalization. These methodological difficulties, the

problem of confidentiality and the late appointment of most evaluators have created a dearth of information about the crucial pilot phase, when project strategies were first formulated. But it could be argued that an evaluator is most apposite at this stage, for by the time the formal trials stage is reached, the commitment to existing strategies may be so strong that the team cannot accept the need for change.

Another undocumented area is what effect the evaluator has on the project team, the teachers and advisory staff. The former would need a 'third party' investigation and has already been alluded to several times. But the effects of the evaluator's informal communication with teachers and advisers, though mentioned in passing by Alexander (1973) and Tawney (1973), may have been an important though unrecognized part of the project's innovation strategy. Even being interviewed or filling in a questionnaire may have encouraged some teachers to reflect on their actions—a second, positive use of the Hawthorne effect which complements the enthusiasm factor noted by Steadman (Chapter 4, p. 64).

Finally, there is the controversial question of a project's public image, which is not mentioned in any of the studies. What do people think it is about? How easily, if at all, can an adverse early image be changed? What effect does it have on subsequent dissemination? Trial schools may not be greatly affected, but if dissemination beyond the trial schools and their immediate locality is wanted, the model of 'image receiver' may be more appropriate than that of 'rational consumer'.

A plea for intrinsic evaluation
The 'rational consumer', who operates according to Stufflebeam's decision-making model (see Chapter 2) and collects information, formulates options and clarifies values, is essentially an ideal type. Nevertheless it is he who is the customer, and without him the provision of information for decision-making can only be a costly waste of time. However, it is possible for the evaluator to give considerable support to the teacher who is neither trained nor given time for elaborate decision-making. In addition to reporting evidence on effects, the evaluator can use intrinsic evaluation (Eraut, 1975) to clarify the assumptions, values and arguments which support the project's curriculum strategy; and to indicate where the project stands on each of the issues which potential adopters might consider important. But if this is not to be perceived as propaganda, it must either be independent of the project itself or else set against a context of alternative strategies. The rational consumer will want to know the main arguments that might be raised against the project and how the project might seek to answer them; and what alternative strategies ought to be considered and what are the significant differences between them. The purpose is to provide a backcloth of possible options, their assumptions, justifications, implications and possible effects, against which the project's curri-

culum strategy and various implementation strategies may be rationally considered.

An intrinsic evaluation of this kind could also have an important formative role, especially if conducted independently and fed back to the project team. It could help point out unnoticed assumptions and alternatives, and forewarn the project of likely criticisms, as well as being a useful document for improving understanding both within the team and between it and the outside world.

Curriculum development, teacher development and in-service education
At the beginning it was pointed out that all the projects under review were involved with problems of innovation as much as with problems of developing new curriculum strategies. Hence we have been concerned not only with curriculum evaluation but also with project evaluation. But is the project to be seen as an innovation in itself or as part of an ongoing, long-term innovation process? Is the evolution of the project's ideas specific in the sense that each school adopts them, adapts them to its own individual circumstances and assimilates them to such an extent that they become part of a new orthodoxy which may be a barrier to future innovation; or is the evolution general, with adoption leading to more rather than less self-evaluation and a greater receptiveness to future innovation? Then, is future innovation perceived as essentially school-based or is another central project expected? Perhaps some kind of dynamic interchange is needed, in which a project draws on school-based innovations, generalizes from them, develops them with a concentrated application of resources and expertise, and then returns them to a wider group of schools with a renewed impetus for further school-based development. The implication of this viewpoint is that in project evaluation one is concerned with the effects of the project in the broadest possible sense, with the dissemination strategy it bequeaths and the state of development of involved schools and LEAs, as well as with the published materials. The question 'To what extent has the project enhanced the capacity of teachers and institutions for self-evaluation and further curriculum development?' then becomes an important criterion.

One factor which emerges from all the evaluation studies is that the need for in-service education was consistently under-estimated. But this usually referred to only one particular type of in-service education, directed at ensuring that the projects' curriculum strategies were properly implemented. The perspective on innovation developed above suggests that other types of in-service education are equally significant, particularly those directed at helping schools to adapt innovations to their own needs and to monitor and evaluate their own progress. Only the Humanities Curriculum Project could be said to have emphasized this need, although many projects appeared to be conscious of it. Then thirdly, and not unrelated to the other two in-service needs, there is the need for in-service education aimed at developing teachers as rational consumers, who make decisions about the adoption, adaption or rejection of project materials and strategies on the basis of their own judgements about pupil needs together, we hope, with the available evidence from evaluation studies. Here, curriculum analysis workshops (Eraut, 1975) are particularly relevant.

The communication of evaluation evidence

Finally there is the problem of communication. Until now we have been discussing what information should be provided to whom, without asking when and how it should be communicated. Nor is this an issue about which any of the evaluators has commented. Science 5–13 and the Humanities Curriculum Project both circulated evaluation reports but mostly only to trial teachers; and the latter project published several papers in learned journals. Only Kelly and Tawney have reported in journals likely to be read by significant numbers of their clients, Kelly in the *Journal of Biological Education* and Tawney in *School Technology*. This review has been based mainly on technical reports prepared for the Schools Council, some of which will have taken as long as three years from completion of draft to publication. The teacher decision-maker may have committed himself long before the information reaches him, and even then it may not be in a digestible form. If the long-term future of curriculum evaluation is dependent on 'consumer education', we seem to have forgotten our customers.

7 Evaluation and the control of education

Barry MacDonald

Evaluators rarely see themselves as political figures, yet their work can be regarded as inherently political, and its varying styles and methods as expressing differing attitudes to the power distribution in education. The evaluator differs from the researcher in that he neither chooses nor controls the enterprise he has to study; his task is not to select questions his instruments can answer, but to find ways of solving questions to which others need answers. He must identify those various, often conflicting groups who make educational decisions and give them the information they feel to be valuable. In choosing his allegiances and priorities, the evaluator necessarily commits himself to a political stance. This chapter offers a political classification of evaluation studies, and ends by considering the contemporary context of such work.

INTRODUCTION

Evaluators seldom if ever talk about themselves as political figures, persons involved in the distribution and exercise of power. To do so would verge on bad taste. Do we not share, with those who teach and those who research and those who administer, a common commitment to the betterment of the educational system we all serve? Let the journalists monitor the tilting balance of control, or talk of 'secret gardens'.* We have a job to do, a technology to perfect, a service to render. Political language is rhetorical or divisive, when it is not both. It is a dangerous discourse for evaluators to engage in.

It is therefore with some trepidation that I address myself to the political dimension of evaluation studies. That I should do so at all is not, as some readers might surmise, because all the legitimate facets of evaluation have been

---

* The phrase 'the secret garden of the curriculum' was coined in 1960 by the then Minister of Education, Sir David Eccles, in the parliamentary debate on the Crowther Report (Central Advisory Council for Education (England), 1959–60). It was a sardonic acknowledgement of the extent to which control of educational policy lay outside national government. The phrase has since become popular with educational journalists.

fully explored in the previous chapters, thus driving me to speculative invention. Rather, it is because I have increasingly come to view evaluation itself as a political activity, and to understand its variety of styles and approaches as expressions of differing stances towards the prevailing distribution of educational power. I intend to propose a simple classification system for evaluation studies. My trepidation will be readily appreciated when I say that the terms I propose to employ are three words which are familiar enough in political discussion, but generally excluded from the vocabulary of dispassionate description: 'bureaucratic', 'autocratic' and 'democratic'. Although it may not be immediately apparent that these are useful words to employ in an interpretative description of evaluation studies, I suggest that we attempt the analysis and see to what extent we feel comfortable with the perspective it generates. Our task is to relate the style of an evaluation study to the political stance it implicitly adopts. The analysis is not intended to be divisive, but to encourage wider reflection on the alternative roles available.

I am aware that only the academic theorist uses these political terms referentially: most of us employ them when we wish to combine a definition of an action or structure with the expression of an attitude towards it. 'Bureaucracy' and 'autocracy' carry overtones of disapproval, while 'democracy'—at least in western societies—can still be relied upon to evoke general approval. Nor am I free from such affective responses myself, and it will not escape the reader that my own stance falls conveniently under the 'democratic' label. Nevertheless, my major argument is not directed against what I shall call bureaucratic and autocratic evaluation stances, but towards the need to make explicit the political orientation of the evaluator, so that we can define the kinds of evaluation study that we want and need. And it may be worth while reminding the reader that we belong to a society which aspires to a form of democracy in which a highly developed bureaucracy is reconciled with individual freedom of action.

Let me begin by giving a historical account of some of the considerations which led me to formulate such a typology. Four occasions stand out in mind. The first was a few years ago, during a visit to the United States. I met a research worker who had recently completed an evaluation of the effects of a particular State school 'bussing' programme. She was in a mood of deep gloom. 'What's the point of educational research?' she said. It turned out that the evaluation report, commissioned by the State authority for a review of its bussing policy, was then ignored when the review took place. The evaluation strongly endorsed the educational value of the prevailing policy, but the decision was to discontinue bussing. The evaluation report was confidential to its sponsors.

I cannot recall how I responded at the time, but now I would say that it was a good piece of educational research but a bad piece of evaluation. Bad for two reasons: first, because it paid insufficient attention to the context of the policy decision it sought to serve and, secondly, because it allowed the conditions of contract to pre-empt the right of those affected to be informed.

A couple of weeks afterwards, I had a brief conversation with one of the most respected exponents of educational evaluation in America, whose views I sought on this issue. He was extremely scathing about the service role adopted by evaluators. A 'cop-out' was what he called it, implying that my new-found profession was little more than the hired help of the bureaucracy. As a Schools Council project evaluator, I found this at the time rather difficult to relate to my own situation. No one, except my mother-in-law and a few well-meaning friends, had told me how to do my job or placed other than financial restrictions on me. I asked this man to tell me how he envisaged the responsibility of evaluation—indeed, how he exercised it, since he was, and still is, a very powerful practitioner. 'It is the duty of the evaluator', he told me, 'to reach a conclusion about the comparative merits of alternative courses of educational action. It is also his duty', he added, 'to ensure that his judgement is implemented by those who control the allocation of resources.'

Taken aback by this remarkably interventionist conception of evaluation, I asked my informant how he could justify such a stance. The answer was twofold. An evaluator's judgement is based on objective evidence of accomplishment—evidence gathered by means of a technology of public procedures and skills. The whole process of conclusion-reaching is guaranteed by the evaluator's peer group, the research community. Muscling in on policy decisions, on the other hand, can be justified by an appeal to democratic principles enshrined in the constitution—principles which the bureaucracy cannot be trusted always to uphold.

I did not find this argument attractive. The 'evaluator king' role appealed to me even less than the role of the 'hired hack'. It seemed to me that the act of evaluation is not value-free. Also, the technology is alarmingly defective, and the whole process of conclusion-reaching far from transparent. What is more, although the research community might be notionally construed as custodian of the scientific detachment of its members, and guarantor of the validity of their conclusions, in fact such a function is only systematically carried out in relation to academic awards. Indeed, the community has shown few signs of any desire to extend that jurisdiction. Perhaps it is just as well. When research is closely related to ideology, as is the case with educational research, history suggests that we lock up the silver.

My third conversation took place more than two years ago, at a gathering of evaluators at Cambridge. This time I can name the other party, something I could not do in the first two instances because I am unsure about the detailed accuracy of my recall, and because it would be wrong to turn casual remarks into enduring statements. We were discussing the role of the evaluator in relation to educational decision-making when Myron Atkin, of the University of Illinois, spelled out what he saw to be a dangerous trend in

America, a growing attempt on the part of the research community to use its authority and prestige to interfere in the political process. It was no part of the researcher's right, *qua* researcher, to usurp the functions of elected office-holders in a democratic society.

I realize that anyone reading this who has a part-time job of evaluating, say, the effect of certain reading materials on children's oral vocabulary in a primary school in Anytown may think this anecdote extremely peripheral to his concerns. I would argue that the underlying issue is one which no evaluator can dismiss and, furthermore, that the resolution of the issue is a major factor in determining his choice of evaluation techniques.

But first my fourth anecdote, involving yet another American. No apology will be called for on that account, I hope, although I anticipate having to resist charges of incipient elitism. We in Britain are fledglings in a specialism that is well established across the Atlantic. Robert Stake was addressing a meeting of the Schools Council evaluators' group at a time of high electoral fever. The then Prime Minister, Edward Heath, had declared the key election issue to be 'Who rules Britain?' and Stake began his presentation by suggesting that an important issue for evaluators was 'Who rules education?' Relating this question to the accountability movement in America (see also below, p. 134), he argued a strong case for recognizing the informational needs of different groups affected by curriculum decisions (see Stake, 1974).

The phrase 'Who rules education?' stuck in my mind, and began to interact with other questions and concerns, including those already mentioned. At that time I had written a couple of things myself that were relevant, and I hope the reader will forgive me for quoting from them. The first was a proposal advocating the funding of an evaluation of computer assisted learning:*

The everyday meaning of the word 'evaluate' is unambiguous. It means quite simply to judge the worth of something. This is a long-established usage, and it is hardly surprising that many people assume that the task of the educational evaluator is to judge the worth of educational programmes. Some evaluators do in fact share this assumption, and a few would even argue that the evaluator has a right to expect that his judgements be suitably reflected in subsequent policy. But there are others, including the present writer, who believe that the proper locus of judgements of worth, and the responsibility for taking them into account in the determination of educational policy, lie elsewhere. In a society such as ours, educational power and accountability are widely dispersed, and situational diversity is a significant factor in educational action. It is also quite clear that our society contains groups and individuals who entertain different, even conflicting, notions of what constitutes educational excellence. The

* 'Educational evaluation of the National Development Programme in Computer Assisted Learning', p. 1. Proposal to the Programme Committee of the National Development Programme, 7 November 1973. The views expressed in the passage quoted are my own. (The proposal appears as Appendix A in *The Programme at Two* (CARE, University of East Anglia, 1975).)

evaluator has therefore many audiences who will bring a variety of perspectives, concerns and values to bear upon his presentations. In a pluralist society, he has no right to use his position to promote his personal values, or to choose which particular educational ideologies he shall regard as legitimate. His job is to identify those who will have to make judgements and decisions about the programme, and to lay before them those facts of the case that are recognised by them as relevant to their concerns.

It did not occur to me when I wrote it that this is an essentially political statement, involving an acknowledgement of the distribution of power and values, an affirmation of a decision-making process, and an assertion of the evaluator's obligation to democratize his knowledge. The second piece I had written introduced a section in a book of readings in curriculum evaluation (Hamilton et al., eds, 1976). The section was concerned to illustrate the 'objectives' model of evaluation and its development from the early papers of Ralph Tyler to current applications in America and Britain. Getting the section ready, I was puzzled still by the difficulty in explaining why this approach to curriculum planning, so popular for so long in America, had really failed to take root in our own country, despite the elegance of its logic and the absence of alternative models. Then it suddenly struck me that the model could be viewed as a cultural artifact, as American as popcorn. It was an ideological model harnessed to a political vision. I wrote:

The inclination of so many American curriculum developers and evaluators to perceive educational change as a technological problem of product specification and manufacture, is by itself unremarkable. Mechanistic analogies have a peculiar appeal for a people who see themselves as the raw materials of a vision which can be socially engineered. Their culture is characteristically forward-looking, constructionist, optimistic and rational. Both the vision and the optimism are reflected in the assumption that goal consensus, a prerequisite of engineering, is a matter of clarification rather than reconciliation. In contrast British culture is nostalgic, conservationist, complacent and distrustful of rationality. Our schools are the agents of continuity, providing discriminating transmission of a culture that has stood the test of time and will continue to do so, given due attention to points of adaptive growth. Goal consensus is neither ardently desired, nor determinedly pursued. Such pursuit would entail a confrontation of value-systems which have so far been contained within an all-embracing rhetoric of generalized educational aims. . . .

The theory and practice of the objectives model of evaluation is thus wedded to an American view of society, and an American faith in technology. Pluralist societies will find it difficult to use. Unified societies will use it, and discover they are pluralist.

Having now aired a number of questions related to the uses and abuses of evaluation from a politico-ideological perspective, I want, before drawing them together, to remind the reader of some crucial distinctions between evaluation and research.

EVALUATION AND RESEARCH

It is possible to emphasize, as Nisbet (1974) did most lucidly at the inaugural meeting of the British Educational Research Association, that curriculum evaluation is an extension of educational research, sharing its roots, using its methods and skills. It was salutary, too, as Nisbet understood, to remind us of the dangers of engaging in our own internecine territorial power games. While I have no wish to quarrel with the assertion of many commonalities shared by evaluation and research, it is important for my present purpose to emphasize one major distinction, and a particular danger in subscribing too readily to the continuity thesis.

The distinction is one to which Hemphill (1969, p. 190) draws attention in a paper on this theme. After stating that the basic and utilitarian purpose of evaluation studies is to provide information for choice among alternatives, and that the choice is a subsequent activity not engaged in by the evaluators, he says:

This fact might lead to the conclusion that an evaluation study could avoid questions of value and utility leaving them to the decision-maker, and thus not need to be distinguished from research, either basic or applied. The crux of the issue, however, is not *who* makes a decision about what alternatives or *what information* serves as the basis for a decision; rather, it is the *degree to which concern with value questions is part and parcel of the study*.

A matter of 'degree' may not suggest a worthwhile distinction. It is necessary to be more explicit. Of course, values enter into research, in a number of ways. There are many people in Britain who have resisted the conclusions of a great deal of educational research since the war, on the grounds of value bias inherent in problem selection and definition. This was notable in the response to research into educational opportunity, and seems likely to characterize the reception of current research in the field of multi-ethnic education. Other value judgements of the researcher are less perceptible and lie buried in his technology. The more esoteric the technology, the less likely are these values to be detected. Test and survey instruments are wrongly assumed to be value-free because of the depersonalized procedures of administration and analysis that govern their application. There is more value bias in research than is commonly recognized. Nevertheless, it remains the responsibility of the researcher to select the problem and devise the means, a responsibility safeguarded by the totem of 'academic freedom'. He construes his task in these terms: 'Which of the questions I judge to be important can I answer with my technology?'

The position of the evaluator is quite distinct, and much more complex. The enterprise he is called upon to study is neither of his choosing nor under his control. He soon discovers, if he has failed to assume it, that his script of educational issues, actions and consequences is being acted out in a socio-political street theatre which affects not just the performance, but the play itself. He finds he can make few assumptions about what has happened, what is happening, or what is going to happen. He is faced with competing interest groups, with divergent definitions of the situation and conflicting informational needs. If he has accepted narrowly stipulative terms of reference, he may find that his options have been pre-empted by contractual restraints that are subsequently difficult to justify. If, on the other hand, he has freedom of action, he faces acute problems. He has to decide which decision-makers he will serve, what information will be of most use, when it is needed and how it can be obtained. I am suggesting that the resolution of these issues commits the evaluator to a political stance, an attitude to the government of education. No such commitment is required of the researcher. He stands outside the political process, and values his detachment from it. For him the production of new knowledge and the social use of that knowledge are rigorously separated. The evaluator is embroiled in the action, built into a political process which concerns the distribution of power, i.e. the allocation of resources and the determination of goals, roles and tasks. And it is naïve to think of educational change as a game in which everybody wins, seductive though that is. One man's bandwagon is another man's hearse.

When evaluation data influence power relationships, the evaluator is compelled to weigh carefully the consequences of his task specification. The much-used term 'independent evaluator' obscures rather than clarifies the problem. Independent of whom? The people who fund the evaluation? The curriculum development team? The pupils, parents, teachers, LEAs, publishers, critics? His own values and needs? The independent evaluator is free only to choose his allegiance, to decide whom he shall listen to, whose questions will be pursued, whose priorities shall have primacy, who has the right to know what. In this sense, the degree of his involvement with values is so much greater than that of the researcher that it amounts to a difference in kind. It also makes explicit the political dimension of evaluation studies.

I said earlier that there was a danger in subscribing too readily to the continuity thesis. It is this. The researcher is free to select his questions, and to seek answers to them. He will naturally select questions which are susceptible to the problem-solving techniques of his craft. In a sense, as Hastings (1969) has pointed out, he uses his instruments to define his problems. The evaluator, on the other hand, must never fall into the error of answering questions which no one but he is asking. He must first identify the significant questions, and only then address the technological problems which they raise. To limit his inquiries to those which satisfy the critical canons of conventional research is to run a serious risk of failing to match the 'vocabulary of action' of the decision-maker, as House has described it (1972, p. 135). The danger, therefore, of conceptualizing evaluation as a branch of research is that evaluators become trapped in the restrictive tentacles of research respectability. Purity may be substituted for utility, trivial proofs for clumsy attempts to grasp complex significance. How much more productive it would be to define research as a branch of evaluation—a branch whose task it is to solve the technological problems encountered by the evaluator.

The relevance of this issue to my present thesis is easy to demonstrate. The political stance of the evaluator has consequences for his choice of techniques for information-gathering and analysis. Recently, I bumped into a researcher whose completed report was being considered for publication at the Schools Council. He was somewhat impatient over a criticism that had been made. 'Some of these people at the Council', he observed caustically, 'seem to think that everything one writes should be understandable to teachers.' This raises the issue nicely. A great deal of new knowledge is produced by researchers and evaluators using techniques and procedures which are difficult to understand. Conclusions are reached and judgements made by the few who are qualified to make them. Others accept or reject these conclusions according to the degree of respect they feel towards those who make them, or the degree to which the conclusions coincide with their beliefs and self-interest.

For many years now, those concerned with the failure of the educational system to make full use of the results of educational research have pleaded for all teachers to be trained in the techniques of research. Perhaps some of that effort should have been expended in exploring techniques that more closely resemble the ways in which teachers normally make judgements— techniques that are more accessible to non-specialist decision-makers. The evaluator who sees his task as feeding the judgement of a range of non-specialist audiences faces the problem of devising such techniques, the problem of trying to respond to the ways of knowing that his audiences use. Such an effort is at present hampered by the subjection of evaluators to a research critique divorced from considerations of socio-political consequences.

A POLITICAL CLASSIFICATION OF EVALUATION STUDIES

Evaluators not only live in the real world of educational politics; they actually influence its changing power relationships. Their work produces information which functions as a resource for the promotion of particular interests and values. Evaluators are committed to a political stance because they must choose between competing claims for this resource. The selection of roles, goals, audiences, issues and techniques by evaluators provides clues to their political allegiance.

It would be useful at this point to describe the three distinct types of evaluation study—bureaucratic, autocratic and democratic. In doing so, I am using the familiar device of ideal typology, that is, describing each type in pure form. When one compares real examples with the ideal, there is rarely a perfect fit, although frequently an approximation can be found. My analysis of ideal types is an attempt to present them equally, to characterize accurately their central features. It would be ironic, however, if I failed to acknowledge that I am hampered in this effort by a personal preference for the 'democratic' stance, and to recognize that an analysis which precedes an argument is always suspect. The field of evaluation has been characterized by studies which fall into one or other of the first two types. The democratic evaluation study is an emerging model, not yet substantially realized, but one which embodies some recent theoretical and practical trends. It is, in part, a reaction to the dominance of the bureaucratic and autocratic types of study currently associated with American programmes.

Bureaucratic evaluation

Bureaucratic evaluation is an unconditional service to those government agencies which have major control over the allocation of educational resources. The evaluator accepts the values of those who hold office, and offers information which will help them to accomplish their policy objectives. He acts as a management consultant, and his criterion of success is client satisfaction. His techniques of study must be credible to the policy-makers and not lay them open to public criticism. He has no independence, no control over the use that is made of his information, and no court of appeal. The report is owned by the bureaucracy and lodged in its files. The key concepts of bureaucratic evaluation are 'service', 'utility' and 'efficiency'. Its key justificatory concept is 'the reality of power'.

Autocratic evaluation

Autocratic evaluation is a conditional service to those government agencies which have major control over the allocation of educational resources. It offers external validation of policy in exchange for compliance with its recommendations. Its values are derived from the evaluator's perception of the constitutional and moral obligation of the bureaucracy. He focuses upon issues of educational merit, and acts as expert adviser. His techniques of study must yield scientific proofs, because his power base is the academic research community. His contractual arrangements guarantee non-interference by the client, and he retains ownership of the study. His report is lodged in the files of the bureaucracy, but is also published in academic journals. If his recommendations are rejected, policy is not validated. His court of appeal is the research community, and high levels in the bureaucracy. The key concepts of the autocratic evaluator are 'principle' and 'objectivity'. His key justificatory concept is 'the responsibility of office'.

*Democratic evaluation**

Democratic evaluation is an information service to the whole community about the characteristics of an educational programme. Sponsorship of the evaluation study does not in itself confer a special claim upon this service. The democratic evaluator recognizes value pluralism and seeks to represent a range of interests in his issue formulation. The basic value is an informed citizenry, and the evaluator acts as broker in exchanges of information between groups who want knowledge of each other. His techniques of data-gathering and presentation must be accessible to non-specialist audiences. His main activity is the collection of definitions of, and reactions to, the pro-gramme. He offers confidentiality to informants and gives them control over his use of the information they provide. The report is non-recommendatory, and the evaluator has no concept of information misuse. He engages in periodic negotiation of his relationships with sponsors and programme par-ticipants. The criterion of success is the range of audiences served. The report aspires to 'best-seller' status. The key concepts of democratic evaluation are 'confidentiality', 'negotiation' and 'accessibility'. The key justificatory con-cept is 'the right to know'.

THE CONTEMPORARY CONTEXT OF EVALUATION STUDIES

What progress can be made towards the task of comparing these ideal types with manifestations in the real world ? It is important to avoid the dangers of labelling and stick to the notion of comparison. To judge by the sudden rash of accountability legislation in the United States, bureaucratic evaluation has American education by the throat, and is tightening its grip. Although it would be an exaggeration to suggest that the long tradition of local control of schools has been seriously undermined, we cannot lightly dismiss the fact that in 1973 thirteen States enacted legislation tying teacher tenure and dismissal to the achievement of performance-based objectives, pre-determined by administrators and assessed by evaluators. Strenuous opposition from teacher unions to this mechanistic over-simplification of complex problems is falling to the argument that soaring educational costs demand proof of payoff. Some observers suspect ulterior motives. House (1973, p. 2) writes: 'I believe such schemes are simplistic, unworkable, contrary to empirical findings, and ulti-mately immoral. They are likely to lead to suspicion, acrimony, inflexibility, cheating, and finally control—which I believe is their real purpose.' If he is correct in this interpretation, and it is at least plausible, then the lack of a professional ethic for evaluators is exposed. This is 'hired help' with a ven-geance, and it gives a wry twist to the Stufflebeam and Guba definition of the

---

* This approach to evaluation is currently guiding field work in the Ford SAFARI Project, which is developing a case-study method of educational inquiry. I am indebted to my colleague Rob Walker, who shares with me responsibility for this conceptualiza-tion.

purpose of evaluation—'aiding and abetting the decision-makers' (1968).

The logic of the accountability movement bears a family resemblance to the engineering paradigm of evaluation pioneered by Tyler and accorded powerful legitimation by the federal bureaucracy in monitoring its massive investment in curriculum development over the past decade, even though the potential of evaluation studies as instruments of control was noted. Cohen (1970, p. 219) writes:

... the Congress is typically of two minds on the matter of program evaluation in education—it subscribes to efficiency, but it does not believe in Federal control of the schools. National evaluations are regarded as a major step toward Federal control by many people, including some members of Congress.

It is also possible to see evidence of autocratic trends in the American evaluation scene. Federal allocation of educational expenditure has always tended to be more sensitive to the need for external validation than policy at the State level, and the expensive national programmes of recent years have seen the rise to powerful advisory positions of evaluators such as Michael Scriven. 'Blue ribbon' panels of evaluation experts are called upon by federal bureaux to decide which of two or more existing programmes should continue to receive support. In this way the bureaucracy controls expenditure and deflects criticism on to the academic 'autocrat'.

What of the democratic model? Some of its cntreal ideas can be detected in the views currently advanced by Stake (1974). Evaluation studies which embody his recognition of value pluralism and multiple audiences will meet some of the criteria of democratic evaluation which I characterized earlier.

Turning to the United Kingdom, the contemporary scene is, in one sense at least, much simpler. If we agree to regard evaluation as distinct from research, then relatively few evaluation studies have been carried out, and only a handful of people would categorize their profession as educational evaluation. Most evaluations have been one-off jobs done by people without prior or subsequent experience, usually teachers on secondment to curriculum projects. We have no evaluation experts. Investment in evaluation studies is marginal at the national level, and almost non-existent at the local level. But that situation could change rapidly. There is concern here too with the rising level of educational expenditure, together with recognition of the need for schools to respond effectively to changing social and economic conditions. These are the conditions of growth for evaluation, which could have a significant role to play in the next decade. What influence will evaluators exert on the changing pattern of control?

The control of education in the United Kingdom has been for half a century vested in a delicately balanced tripartite system, with power shared between central government, local government and teachers. The composition and terms of reference of the Schools Council maintain this balance carefully enough to reflect the strength of the ideal or the zealousness with which the partners guard their share of control. Despite its relatively small budget and its limited powers, the Council is regarded with some suspicion by those who fear bids for more control of education by national government. The Council came into being as a result of teacher reaction to ministry initiatives, and it is located in London, originally within a stone's throw of the Department of Education and Science. Stones have been known to carry instructions! Others argue that the Council is more vulnerable to control by the teacher unions, by virtue of their superior representation. It could become a practitioner bureaucracy. The Council is a microcosm of the convergences and divergences of interest in the government of education. Developments in its control and objectives will have implications for evaluation studies. Up to the present, Council evaluators have enjoyed a remarkable degree of freedom in the conduct of their work, although the Council exercises some degree of control over publication.

A less parochial perspective reveals that one of the most striking contemporary educational events in western industrialized societies is the forceful intervention of national government in the affairs of the school. Effective curriculum development has become an internationally recognized need, and evaluation will be a sought-after service in this effort. Evaluation costs money, and those who commission evaluation studies will be those who command resources. Who will serve the powerless if the evaluator flies the 'gold standard' (Stake, 1976, Chapter 20)? The independent foundations like Nuffield, Gulbenkian and Leverhulme may have an even more important role to play in the future than they have had in the past. Although their American equivalents have come under attack recently, accused variously of conservative conceptualizations, political meddling and ineptness, the independent sponsors may fulfil the need for checks and balances in changing power relationships.

One final point. The boundaries between educational and social programmes are becoming increasingly blurred; nursery provision, ethnic education and compensatory programmes are prime examples. Values seem likely to enter increasingly into the considerations of evaluators. There will be a place in the future for the three types of evaluation study outlined here, but there may be a special case for exploring in practice some of the principles which characterize the democratic model. For those who believe that means are the most important category of ends, it deserves refutation or support.

Appendix
Some instruments used in evaluation
Stephen Steadman and John Hayter

This appendix presents a few selected examples of the instruments described in Chapter 4. They are drawn from the Continuing Mathematics Project, where trials are being organized by the evaluator, John Hayter.

The project has been producing programmed learning materials, supported by tape-slide sequences, experiments and games, intended for sixth form level students who are not taking mathematics as a main study but who need to continue their mathematics. The material is structured into units, each unit taking an average student from two to three hours to work. The units are self-instructional and suitable for use by individuals or small groups. Some units cover basic O level topics and are intended as 'service' units; others, such as those dealing with critical path analysis, are independent; while sequences of units make up courses in probability and statistics, and calculus.

Developing the materials involves three stages of trials:

(a) developmental testing with small numbers of students in schools near the project's base;
(b) field testing with 100–200 students in schools and colleges across the country;
(c) validation trials in a large number of institutions prior to publication.

Both before and after the developmental testing, the views of external moderators are sought.

The selection of documents presented here is seen very much out of context. If the questions posed and the scales used seem direct, unsophisticated, even crude at times, it should be remembered that the answers obtained are not the only source of the evaluator's information. A number of questions are followed up in interviews. Some questions reflect general concerns of the project, while others are highly specific to the individual pupil task under review. Invariably some kind of cross-check has been applied to the information.

The following statement of the aims of the evaluation was prepared for a conference of trial tutors at Easter in 1974:

NOTES ON THE EVALUATION OF THE CONTINUING MATHEMATICS
PROJECT

... A number of factors can be identified as influencing the desired nature and methods of evaluation. Four of these are (i) the independent use of the materials by students, without the interpretive role of a teacher; (ii) the necessity for inbuilt testing to provide students with a measure of their progress; (iii) the non-existence of a slot in the sixth form curriculum for the study of more mathematics; and (iv) the unfamiliarity of self-instructional work for the majority of students.

The project is therefore concerned not with introducing new ideas and materials into a situation which is well understood but rather with preparing a relatively untried approach to teaching fairly familiar material. This takes place in a context which is varied and complex, involving not only the state of the curriculum structure but also the attitudes of teachers across a range of subjects in a given institution. The task of the evaluator is therefore seen in terms of an inside adviser to the team (often it seems in the form of chief problem poser!) rather than as a freelance independent judge. This is not to deny the possible value of an independent evaluation at a later stage.

The three major aims of the evaluation are seen at present to be:

1. To provide information for the further development of materials by means of
   (a) developmental testing of materials—team members working closely with small groups of students;
   (b) field testing of materials—(i) collection and analysis of student work sheets, tests and feedback sheets from a number of schools and colleges with teachers acting as tutors; (ii) interviews with students and tutors; and (iii) collection of opinions of tutors and other specialists on suitability of materials for stated objectives;
   (c) clarification of mathematical needs of students—(i) discussions with subject specialists in schools, colleges, universities and industry; (ii) discussion with students in sixth forms and higher education; and (iii) contacts with GCE examining boards concerning the development of a more quantified approach within a number of 'A' level syllabuses;
   (d) investigation of possibilities for use of such self-instructional materials in schools and colleges, in order to obtain a greater understanding of the timetable, motivational and mundane practical problems which exist.
2. To provide a measure of the effectiveness of the teaching materials by means of validation testing to take place in 1974 prior to publication. In addition to considering the achievement of content objectives, attention will be given to student attitudes to mathematics in general and these materials in particular.
3. To provide a statement concerning the opportunities, problems and experiences of using self-instructional materials for teaching mathematics to non-specialists. Such a study to contribute to the establishment of a strategy for the dissemination phase.

EXTERNAL MODERATION OF UNITS

The project issued the following notes for moderators:

Each unit of work produced by the project is normally prepared by a member of the team assisted at the outline and draft stages by one or two colleagues who act as 'internal' moderators. Following changes which take place after moderation, the unit is used by 10–20 students in local schools (developmental testing) and then, after further revision, by up to 200 students in a variety of schools and colleges (field testing).

It is seen to be highly desirable that each unit should be exposed to an outside moderator. Such a person would be in a position to look at the unit in a fresh way, using the knowledge and experience which he or she has, to comment on the soundness of the mathematics and the clarity of the exposition, and to show, by making suggestions on re-wording, how a point can be made more vividly or a concept better driven home.

In order to provide some guidance on the areas on which the project team would value comment, an outline specification is indicated below. Needless to say it is not intended to be restrictive, and moderators should feel free to make additional comments if they feel them appropriate.

Stage 1 (developmental testing version of the unit)
The moderation to provide comments

  (*a*) on the clarity of the teaching strategy;
  (*b*) on the 'soundness' of the mathematical content;
  (*c*) on the consistency of the objectives, the content of the unit and the post-test items;
  (*d*) on the relative contributions of the components of the unit (text, tape/filmstrip, etc.);
  (*e*) on the suitability of the content and style for the target population of students (sixth formers or college or university students not specializing in mathematics);
  (*f*) in detail, on the frames comprising the text or filmstrip.

Notes on any apparent deficiencies in coverage together with any general, or—even better—detailed suggestions for improvement would also be helpful.

Stage 2 (field testing version of the unit)
To cover the same ground as Stage 1 but hopefully in a briefer form. (An author will normally have discussed any points of disagreement with the moderator when revising the first version.)

In addition, where a sequence of units is being considered, comments on (*a*) the relationship between sequential units, and (*b*) the completeness of the sequence content, would be of great value.

It is hoped that moderators would normally be able to provide their written reports within one month of receiving the units.

INSTRUMENTS FOR DATA COLLECTION

Forms A and B (pp. 141 and 142) are examples of instruments used to collect comments from tutors on individual units, Form A at the developmental stage of testing and Form B at the field testing stage. Space does not permit the inclusion of examples of the forms intended to collect comments upon the sequences of units used together as a course. Most of the questions shown ask for unstructured, open responses. This should be compared with the later students' feedback forms (C to E). The difference is partly explained by the fact that the evaluator can reasonably expect to interview almost every tutor to follow up comments.

Forms C, D and E (pp. 144, 146 and 147) are designed to collect student feedback. Form C, in use, is part of the actual answer booklet to the unit on 'Flowcharts and algorithms', together with the pre- and post-tests not shown here. Form D has been designed to examine response to an introductory unit presented together with a tape-slide sequence. Form E asks for reactions to an experiment suggested to students as part of their work on a unit.

The last item in these selected examples of feedback instruments is a work diary (Form F, p. 148) on which tutors record pupils' progress with the units of work. The form of recording required was kept brief to minimize the time required for completion by a tutor. Yet the coding retains sufficient information to be useful. For instance, the mythical Charles Macpie spent $1\frac{1}{2}$ weeks (three 35 minute periods) working through unit A of the probability course and the next period doing experiment 1.1. It was from such returns as these from tutors that the project was alerted to the students' tendency to 'bog down' if left to work entirely alone.

Limitations of space do not permit a full collection of the forms used in this evaluation programme to be presented. Items not reproduced here include:

the pre- and post-tests which are part of each unit;
the institution profile asking for information about the school, the group of students and the facilities they have;
the student information sheet, which asks for details of qualifications, course of study, career plans and mathematical needs;
questionnaires upon complete courses of units;
students' answer booklets;
personal record sheets for tutors and students.

It should also be noted that the layout of the examples shown as Forms A to F has been modified for inclusion in this publication.

Form A   Continuing Mathematics Project: tutor's report form on
developmental testing

(To be forwarded to unit author with answer booklets, etc.)

Unit: .... Tutor: ....

Number of students using unit: ....

Nature of group (school/college; year of study; main subject interest);
....
....

Additional information about students (as individuals or group) if
any: ....
....
....

Conditions of use (private study/supervised by tutor, etc.):
....
....

Particular circumstances which affected use of materials (e.g. unsuitable
room, students visiting school doctor, etc.):
....
....

If used during regular timetable, how many sessions were necessary to
complete the unit? ....
....

Materials accompanying this report as follows:
student answer booklets: ....
other evidence: ....

Were there any problems in administering the materials which make up
the unit? ....
....

On which parts did students require most help? ....
....
....

How did students react to this unit? ....
....

General remarks about students' progress with the unit: ....
....
....

Tutor's own comments on the unit: ....
....
....

Form B Continuing Mathematics Project: tutor's comment form on 'Further Critical Path Analysis'

This form is in three parts:

Part A to be used as a jotting pad to note ideas, problems and difficulties as they arise;

Part B a short questionnaire on the suitability of the unit for the students and on the unit's performance in general;

Part C an opportunity for the tutor to comment on the unit from his specialist standpoint. Remarks on the content, the teaching strategy, use of media, etc. will be welcomed.

Name of tutor: .... Subject: ....

School: ....

PART A

Notes on problems arising during the students' use of the unit.
[$\frac{1}{2}$ page left for comments]

PART B

1. How many students used the unit? ......

2. In what context was the unit used? (e.g. General Studies, 'A' level Biology course, etc.) ....
....

3. Did the students use the unit
   on a classroom basis? ☐
   on an individual basis at home? ☐
   in the library/resource centre? ☐

4. Did the students study this unit immediately after working the first unit N_A?...
....

5. Were all students in the group required to use the unit or did students choose to do it after meeting the ideas of Critical Path Analysis in N_A? ....
....

[cont.]

6. Did you give any specific directions to your students on the use of the optional section on 'early' and 'late' event times?
....
....

7. Our developmental testing of the unit indicated that while some students thoroughly enjoyed the calculations of event times, others found it irksome. Hence the decision at this stage to make the section optional, students already having learned a method for calculating float. From the experience of the unit with your students, how successful do you judge this strategy to be?
....
....

8. Do you consider that, as a result of using this unit, the interest of the majority of your students in Critical Path Analysis was increased/sustained/lessened? ....
....

9. What were the chief difficulties experienced by the students in using the unit? ....
....

10. Does the experience of your group of students indicate any changes that need to be made to the length, format, construction of the unit? ....
....

PART C

We shall greatly value your comments as a teacher on the content and approach used in the unit. If a Mathematics specialist, you will clearly view it somewhat differently from a Biology or Chemistry specialist who may simply want students to operate efficiently with a mathematical tool. The views of those with differing subject specialisms will be equally welcomed by the project team.
[page left for comments]

Thank you for your help.

Form C Continuing Mathematics Project: student's feedback form on 'Flowcharts and Algorithms' (from the unit's answer booklet)

We shall appreciate your comments on the unit you have just completed.

1. How long did you spend working on this unit?   ...... mins

2. Please indicate in the table below the parts of the unit which you used and the time you spent on each part.

	Yes/no Time (mins)
'Flowcharts and Algorithms' text Appendix Part A: 'Write-a-Story' Part B: 'Some notes on the game' Post-test	

3. Which part of the unit (if any) did you enjoy most?
   ....
   ....

4. Which part (if any) did you find difficult?
   ....
   ....

5. Did you find any part of the unit boring? If so, please indicate which part. ....
   ....

6. If you played 'Write-a-Story',
   (a) how many played with you?   ......
   (b) did you find the game
       very enjoyable/enjoyable/rather boring/very boring/don't know?
   (c) did you find it a helpful illustration of 'Flowcharts'?
                                              Yes/no/don't know
   (d) did you listen to a tape describing the game?   *Yes/no*
       If so, (i) did you find the commentary on the tape easy to follow?
                                              Yes/no/not sure
              (ii) did you find the introduction to the game on tape
                   very helpful/fairly helpful/unnecessary/confusing?
   (e) would you like to play the game again?   *Yes/no/don't know*

7. In general I found
   (i) the pace of the text:
       much too fast/rather fast/about right/rather slow/much too slow;
   (ii) the mathematical ideas:
       very clear/fairly clear/not quite clear/very unclear;
   (iii) this text:
       very boring/rather boring/fairly interesting/very interesting;
   (iv) the work:
       very difficult/quite difficult/about right/quite easy/very easy.

[cont.]

8. What do you consider you have gained by studying this unit?

   ....

   ....

9. Having studied this introductory unit, would you like to learn more about any of the topics in the unit? (Specify by name or by page number any topics which particularly interest you.)

   ....

   ....

10. Having spent some time working on the unit, you may have some suggestions for improving the unit. Please write any such suggestions below.
    [$\frac{1}{2}$ page left for comments]

P ease return the answer booklet to your tutor.

Form D Continuing Mathematics Project: student's comment form on 'Setting the Probability Scene'

School/college .... Date ....

1. Did you listen to the tape more than once?   *Yes/no*

2. Did you think that the presenter spoke
   (i) too slowly,
   (ii) at the right pace,
   (iii) too quickly?   ....

3. Did you think that the amount of material in the tape was
   (i) too little,
   (ii) about right,
   (iii) too much?   ....

4. Were you able to follow the references to the various parts of your leaflet and still follow the programme?   *Yes/no*

5. Do you remember any part of the tape which was difficult to follow? If so, which part? ....
   ....

6. How long did you spend in studying pp. 1, 2 of your leaflet *after* listening to the tape?   ...... mins

7. Do you think the material on p. 1 of your leaflet helped you to remember the stages in the tape presentation?   *Yes/no*

8. Did you find the post-test
   (i) easy,
   (ii) about right,
   (iii) difficult,
   (iv) very difficult?   ....

9. How many of the (5) questions in the post-test were you able to answer correctly?   ....

10. Which questions, if any, did you find difficult to answer?
    ....
    ....

11. Copy your choices of the correct options in the post-test in the [spaces] below.
    Q. 1 ......   Q. 2 ......   Q. 3 ......   Q. 4 ......   Q. 5 ......

Form E Continuing Mathematics Project: student's comment form on 'Statistical Experiments'

Name .... School ....
Experiment .... Time spent on experiment ....

1. Were you able to decide on the purpose of the experiment by reading the outline description? If not, what did you find difficult in the description? ....
....

2. Were you able to decide on your approach simply from the outline description? *Yes/no*

3. Did you modify your approach after reading the procedure of page 2? *Yes/no*

4. If you needed more help, did you use
   (a) the procedure of page 2? *Yes/no*
   (b) the detailed method of page 4? *Yes/no*
   (c) some other advice? *Yes/no*
   If you answer (c) with *yes*, what help did you receive?
   ....
   ....

5. Can you suggest any way in which the procedure on the second page might be made clearer? ....
   ....

6. Can you suggest any way in which the detailed method on the fourth page might be made clearer? ....
   ....

7. There are three parts to the carrying out of the experiment. Collecting and recording data, making graphs, doing calculations. Rate each one, under the headings provided, according to how interesting you found it.

	Tedious & boring	Tedious	Quite interesting	Very interesting
(i) Data				
(ii) Graphs				
(iii) Calculation				

Put a √ in the appropriate [spaces].

8. When you had collected, recorded, and presented the data and had made some calculations, were you able to draw any conclusions from your results? *Yes/no*

9. Can you suggest an experiment which is no more difficult to carry out and which needs no more knowledge which would be of more interest to you? ....
   ....

Form F Continuing Mathematics Project: extract from tutor's record sheet

Notes: 1. Information on progress from Student Record Sheet.
2. At the end of weeks marked with X's please return copy of this record sheet to University of Sussex.

School: .... Tutor: ....

Student's name	Time per week	Week ending						
		(1)	(2)		(3)	(4)	(5)	(6)
Charles Macpie	2×35 mins	$P_A \rightarrow$	P_A	Exp 1.1	$P_{BI} \rightarrow$ X	$P_{BI} \rightarrow$	Exp 1.5	P_C	$P_C \rightarrow$ X
					X				X
					X				X

References

Adams, G. S., and Torgerson, T. L. (1964). *Measurement and Evaluation in Education, Psychology and Guidance*. New York: Holt, Rinehart.

Adams, R. N., and Preiss, J. J., eds (1960). *Human Organization Research: Field Relations and Techniques*. Homewood, Ill.: Dorsey Press.

Ahmann, J. S., and Glock, M. D. (1958). *Evaluating Pupil Growth: Principles of Tests and Measurements*. Boston: Allyn & Bacon.

Alexander, D. J. (1973). 'Nuffield Secondary Science', pp. 177–83 in *Evaluation in Curriculum Development: Twelve Case Studies* (Schools Council Research Studies). Macmillan Education.

—— (1974). *Nuffield Secondary Science: an Evaluation* (Schools Council Research Studies). Macmillan Education.

Alkin, M. C. (1970). 'Products for improving educational evaluation', *Evaluation Comment*, **2** (3), 1–15.

—— (1972). 'Wider context goals and goal-based evaluators', *Evaluation Comment*, **3** (4), 6–7.

Anastasi, A. (1968). *Psychological Testing*. 3rd ed. New York: Macmillan.

Anstey, E. (1966). *Psychological Tests*. Nelson.

Bannister, D., and Mair, J. M. M. (1968). *The Evaluation of Personal Constructs*. Academic Press.

Bealing, D. (1973). 'Issues in classroom observational research', *Research in Education*, **9** (May), 70–82.

Becker, H. S., Geer, B., and Hughes, E. C. *Making the Grade: the Academic Side of College Life*. New York and Chichester: John Wiley.

Bloom, B. S., ed. (1956). *Taxonomy of Educational Objectives: the Classification of Educational Goals*, Handbook 1: *Cognitive Domain*. Longmans.

Blyth, W. A. L., et al. (1972). *An Interim Statement*. Schools Council project on History, Geography and Social Science 8–13, based at the University of Liverpool School of Education from 1971.

Bradfield, J. M., and Moredock, H. S. (1957). *Measurement and Evaluation in Education*. New York: Macmillan.

Brimer, M. A. (1967). 'An experimental evaiuation of coded scripts in initial reading', *New Research in Education*, **1**, 124–9.

—— (1968). 'The classification of qualitative data'. University of Bristol School of Education (unpublished).

Bruner, J. S. (1966). *Toward a Theory of Instruction*. Cambridge, Mass.: Harvard University Press (Belknap Press).

Buros, O. K., ed. (1972). *The Seventh Mental Measurements Yearbook*. Highland Park, NJ: Gryphon Press.

Burstall, C., et al. (1974). *Primary French in the Balance*. Slough: National Foundation for Educational Research.

Butcher, H. J. (1966). *Sampling in Educational Research*. Manchester University Press.

Campbell, D. T., and Stanley, J. C. (1963). *Experimental and Quasi-Experimental Designs for Research*. Chicago: Rand McNally.

Caro, F. G. (1971). 'Issues in the evaluation of social programs', *Review of Educational Research*, **41**, 87–114.

Central Advisory Council for Education (England) (1959–60). *15 to 18* [Crowther Report]. 2 vols. HMSO.

—— (1967). *Children and their Primary Schools* [Plowden Report]. 2 vols. HMSO.

Cicourel, A. V. (1964). *Method and Measurement in Sociology*. New York: Free Press.

Clegg, A. (1968). 'Improving methods of communication and implementation', p. 28 in *Curriculum Innovation in Practice*, ed. J. S. Maclure. HMSO.

Close, J. J., Rudd, A. W. G., and Plimmer, F. (1974). *Team Teaching Experiments*. Slough: National Foundation for Educational Research.

Clymer, T. (1972). 'What is "reading"?: some current concepts', pp. 48–66 in *Reading Today and Tomorrow*, by A. Melnik and J. Merritt. University of London Press. (Reprinted from pp. 7–29 of *Innovation and Change in Reading Instruction*, ed. H. M. Robinson (67th Yearbook of the National Society for the Study of Education). University of Chicago Press, 1968.)

Cochran, W. G. (1963). *Sampling Techniques*. 2nd ed. London: Wiley.

Cohen, D. K. (1970). 'Politics and research: evaluation of social action programs in education', *Review of Educational Research*, **40** (2), 213–38.

Cook, D. L. (1962). 'The Hawthorne Effect in educational research', *Phi Delta Kappan*, December, 116–22.

Cronbach, L. J. (1960). *Essentials of Psychological Testing*. New York: Harper.

—— (1963). 'Course improvement through evaluation', *Teachers College Record*, **64** (8), 672–83.

Cronbach, L. J., and Suppes, P. (1969). *Research for Tomorrow's Schools: Disciplined Inquiry for Education*. New York: Macmillan.

Crossland, R. W. (1967). 'Report of an individual study of the Nuffield Foundation Primary Science Project'. University of Manchester (unpublished).

Crossland, R. W., and Moore, S. F. D. (1974). *Environmental Studies Project (5–13): an Evaluation* (Schools Council Research Studies). Macmillan Education.

Dennien, R. T., et al. (1973). 'Devising evaluation instruments for technological problem solving', *Journal of Curriculum Studies*, **5** (2), 122–32.

Downing, J. A., ed. (1967). *The i.t.a. Symposium*. London: National Foundation for Educational Research.

Eggleston, J. F., Galton, M. J., and Jones, M. E. (1975). *A Science Teaching Observation Schedule* (Schools Council Research Studies). Macmillan Education.

Eraut, M. R. (1972). *In-service Education for Innovation* (National Council for Educational Technology Occasional Paper 4). Councils and Education Press.

Eraut, M. R., Goad, L. H., and Smith, G. E. (1975). *The Analysis of Curriculum Materials*. Education Area, University of Sussex (Occasional Paper 2).

Fleming, W. (1973/4). 'An exercise in evaluation', *Newsmaths*, 8 (winter), 8–11 (journal of the Schools Council Mathematics for the Majority Continuation Project, based at 3 The Cloisters, Cathedral Close, Exeter, from 1971 to 1975).

Flynn, J. M. (1972). 'Evaluation and the fate of innovations', *Educational Technology*, April, 52–4.

Forehand, G. A. (1970). 'Curriculum evaluation as decision-making process', *Journal of Research and Development in Education*, 3, 27–37.

Gallagher, J. J. (1970). 'Three studies of the classroom', pp. 74–108 in *Classroom Observation*, by J. J. Gallagher, G. A. Nuthall and B. Rosenshine (American Educational Research Association Monograph on Curriculum Evaluation no. 6). Chicago: Rand McNally.

Glaser, B. G., and Strauss, A. L. (1967). *The Discovery of Grounded Theory: Strategies of Qualitative Research*. Weidenfeld & Nicolson.

Glaser, R. (1970). 'Evaluation of instruction and changing educational models', p. 75 in *Problems in the Evaluation of Instruction*, ed. M. C. Wittrock and D. E. Wiley. New York: Holt, Rinehart.

Glass, G. V., and Worthen, B. R. (1972). 'Educational inquiry and the practice of education', pp. 68–123 in *Conceptual Frameworks for Viewing Educational Research, Development, Diffusion, and Evaluation* (*The Oregon Studies in Educational Research, Development, Diffusion, and Evaluation*, vol. III), ed. H. del Schalock and G. R. Sell. Monmouth, Oregon: Teaching Research Division, Oregon State System of Higher Education.

Grobman, H. (1968). *Evaluation Activities of Curriculum Projects: a Starting Point* (American Educational Research Association Monograph on Curriculum Evaluation no. 2). Chicago: Rand McNally.

—— (1972). 'Content analysis in formative and summative evaluation of curriculum'. Paper presented to an international symposium on Evaluation in Science Education and Uses of Educational Technology, at the fourth biennial meeting of the Asian Association for Biological Education, Jerusalem, August.

Gronlund, N. E. (1965). *Measurement and Evaluation in Teaching*. New York: Macmillan.

Guilford, J. P. (1959). 'Three faces of intellect', *American Psychologist*, 14, 469–70.

Guttentag, M. (1971). 'Models and methods in evaluation research', *Journal of the Theory of Social Behavior*, 1, 75–95.

Hamilton, D. F., and Delamont, S. (1974). 'Classroom research: a cautionary tale', *Research in Education*, 11 (May), 1–16.

Hamilton, D. F., et al., eds (1976). *Reader in Illuminative Evaluation*. Berkeley, Calif.: McCutchan.

Hamingson, D., ed. (1973). *Towards Judgement*. An edited compilation of the publications of the evaluation unit of the Schools Council Humanities Curriculum Project, 1970–2 (mimeo). Norwich: Centre for Applied Research in Education, University of East Anglia (CARE Occasional Publication no. 1).

Hanley, J. P., et al. (1969). *Curiosity, Competence, Community*. Cambridge, Mass.: Educational Development Center.

Harlen, W. (1967). *An Evaluation of the Development of Scientific Concepts in Children Taking Part in the Oxford Primary Science Research Project (1966–67)*. Bristol: Research Unit, University of Bristol Institute of Education.

—— (1973). 'Science 5–13 Project', pp. 16–35 in *Evaluation in Curriculum Development: Twelve Case Studies* (Schools Council Research Studies). Macmillan Education.

—— (1975). *Science 5–13: a Formative Evaluation* (Schools Council Research Studies). Macmillan Education.

Hastings, J. T. (1966). 'Curriculum evaluation: the why of the outcomes', *Journal of Educational Measurement*, **3** (1), 27–32.

—— (1969). 'The kith and kin of educational measurers', *Journal of Educational Measurement*, **6** (3), 127–30.

Hays, W. L. (1970). *Statistics*. 2 vols. New York: Holt, Rinehart.

Helmstadter, G. C. (1966). *Principles of Psychological Measurement*. Methuen.

Hemphill, J. K. (1969). 'The relationship between research and evaluation studies', pp. 189–220 in *Educational Evaluation: New Roles, New Means*, ed. R. W. Tyler (68th Yearbook of the National Society for the Study of Education). University of Chicago Press.

Henry, J. (1971). *Essays on Education*. Harmondsworth: Penguin.

Herndon, J. H. (1965). *The Way it Spozed to Be*. New York: Simon & Schuster.

Holt, J. (1964). *How Children Fail*. New York: Dell (new ed. Pitman, 1970).

House, E. R. (1972). 'The conscience of educational evaluation', *Teachers College Record*, **73** (3), 405–14.

—— (1973). *The Price of Productivity: Who Pays?* Urbana-Champaign, Ill.: University of Illinois (mimeo).

Hyman, H. H., et al. (1954). *Interviewing in Social Research*. University of Chicago Press (reprinted 1962).

Ikin, A. E. (1944). *The Education Act*. Pitman.

Jackson, P. W. (1968). *Life in Classrooms*. New York: Holt, Rinehart.

Jenkins, D. (1973). 'Integrated Studies Project', pp. 70–9 in *Evaluation in Curriculum Development: Twelve Case Studies* (Schools Council Research Studies). Macmillan Education.

Kaner, P. (1973). 'Mathematics for the Majority Project', pp. 128–46 in *Evaluation in Curriculum Development: Twelve Case Studies* (Schools Council Research Studies). Macmillan Education.

Kelly, G. A. (1955). *The Psychology of Personal Constructs*, vol. 1. New York: Norton.

Kelly, P. J. (1971a). 'The process of curriculum innovation', pp. 84–106 in *Paedagogica Europaea*, vol. VI (1970/71): *The Changing School Curriculum in Europe*. The Hague: Malmberg/Brunswick: Westermann.

—— (1971b). 'Evaluation studies of the Nuffield A-level biology trials, 1: Overall achievements of students', *Journal of Biological Education*, **5**, 315 –27.

—— (1972a). 'Evaluation studies of the Nuffield A-level biology trials, 2: Evaluation of specific objectives', *Journal of Biological Education*, **6**, 29–40.

—— (1972b). 'Evaluation studies of the Nuffield A-level biology trials, 3: Student characteristics and achievement', *Journal of Biological Education*, **6**, 99–107.

—— (1972c). 'Evaluation studies of the Nuffield A-level biology trials, 4: School characteristics and achievement', *Journal of Biological Education*, **6**, 197–205.

—— (1972d). 'Evaluation studies of the Nuffield A-level biology trials, 5: Students after the trials', *Journal of Biological Education*, **6**, 259–66.

—— (1973a). 'Nuffield A Level Biological Science Project', pp. 91–109 in *Evaluation in Curriculum Development: Twelve Case Studies* (Schools Council Research Studies). Macmillan Education.

—— (1973b). 'Early stages in the diffusion of the Nuffield A-level biology project', *Journal of Biological Education*, **9**, 15–22.

Kerr, J. F., ed. (1968). *Changing the Curriculum*. University of London Press (reprinted 1970).

Kitchen, R. D. (1970). 'The semantic differential and value judgements of student teachers', *Educational Research*, **12** (2), 150–3.

Kourilsky, M. (1973). 'An adversary model for educational evaluation', *Evaluation Comment*, **4** (2), 3–6.

Kuhn, T. S. (1970). *The Structure of Scientific Revolutions*. 2nd ed. University of Chicago Press.

Larsson, I. (1973). *Individualized Mathematics Teaching*. Stockholm: Lund-Berlingska Boktyckerier.

Laughton, W. H., and Wilkinson, W. J. (1968). 'Pupils' attitudes to science teaching', *Education in Science*, **26**, 31–3.

Lewis, D. G. (1968). *Experimental Design in Education*. University of London Press.

Lewy, A. (1973). 'The practice of curriculum evaluation', *Curriculum Theory Network*, **11** (spring), 6–33.

Light, R. J., and Smith, P. V. (1970). 'Choosing a future: strategies for designing and evaluating new programs', *Harvard Educational Review*, **40** (winter), 1–28.

Lindvall, C. M., and Cox, R. C. (1970). *Evaluation as a Tool in Curriculum Development: the IPI Evaluation Program* (American Educational Research Association Monograph on Curriculum Evaluation no. 5). Chicago: Rand McNally.

McCall, G. J., and Simmons, J. L., eds (1969). *Issues in Participant Observation*. Reading, Mass.: Addison-Wesley.

MacDonald, B. (1971). 'The evaluation of the Humanities Curriculum Project: a holistic approach', *Theory into Practice*, **10** (3), 163–7.

—— (1973). 'Humanities Curriculum Project', pp. 80–90 in *Evaluation in Curriculum Development: Twelve Case Studies* (Schools Council Research Studies). Macmillan Education.

Maclure, J. S., ed. (1968). *Curriculum Innovation in Practice*. Report of the

Third International Curriculum Conference, Oxford, 17–22 September 1967. HMSO.

Medley, D. M., and Mitzel, H. E. (1963). 'Measuring classroom behavior by systematic observation', pp. 247–328 in *Handbook of Research on Teaching*, ed. N. L. Gage. Chicago: Rand McNally.

Messick, S. (undated). *Evaluation of Educational Programs as Research on Educational Process*. Princeton, NJ: Educational Testing Service.

Moser, C. A. (1967). *Survey Methods in Social Investigation*. Heinemann Educational Books.

Nash, R. (1973). *Classrooms Observed*. Routledge.

Nisbet, J. D. (1974). 'Educational research—the state of the art'. Paper presented at the inaugural meeting of the British Educational Research Association, 5 April in Manchester (unpublished).

Nottingham, B. (1970). 'The measurement of pupils' attitudes', *Educational Research*, **12** (3), 247–9.

Nuthall, G. A. (1970). 'A review of some selected studies of classroom inter-action and teaching behavior', pp. 6–29 in *Classroom Observation*, by J. J. Gallagher, G. A. Nuthall and B. Rosenshine (American Educational Research Association Monograph on Curriculum Evaluation no. 6). Chicago: Rand McNally.

Nuttall, D. L., and Willmott, A. S. (1972). *British Examinations: Techniques of Analysis*. Slough: National Foundation for Educational Research.

Ober, R. L., Bentley, E. L., and Miller, E. (1971). *Systematic Observation of Teaching*. Englewood Cliffs, NJ: Prentice-Hall.

Ogilvie, E. (1974). 'Creativity and curriculum structure', *Educational Research*, **16** (2), 126–32.

Oppenheim, A. N. (1966). *Questionnaire Design and Attitude Measurement*. Heinemann Educational Books (reprinted 1973).

Organisation for Economic Co-operation and Development, Centre for Educational Research and Innovation (1971). *Innovation in Education: Sweden* (by J. S. Maclure); *Germany* (by H. Thomas); *Norway* (by P. Dalin); *United States* (by L. Sussmann with M. O'Brien); *England* (by A. Corbett). Paris: OECD (mimeo, ref. CERI/EI/71.02 to 71.06, June).

Osgood, C. E., Suci, G. J., and Tannenbaum, P. H. (1957). *The Measurement of Meaning*. Urbana, Ill.: University of Illinois Press (new ed. 1968).

Parlett, M. R. (1967). 'Classroom and beyond: a study of a sophomore physics section at MIT'. Cambridge, Mass.: Education Research Center, Massachusetts Institute of Technology (unpublished).

—— (1969). 'Undergraduate teaching observed', *Nature*, **223**, 1102–1104.

—— (1971). 'Study of two experimental programs at MIT'. Cambridge, Mass.: Education Research Center, Massachusetts Institute of Technology (unpublished).

—— (1972). 'Evaluating innovations in teaching', pp. 144–154 in *Contemporary Problems in Research in Higher Education*, ed. H. J. Butcher and E. Rudd. McGraw-Hill.

Parlett, M. R., and King, J. G. (1971). *Concentrated Study: a Pedagogic Inno-*

vation Observed (Research in Higher Education Monograph no. 14). London: Society for Research in Higher Education.

Perry, W. G. (1970). *Forms of Intellectual and Ethical Development in the College Years*. New York: Holt, Rinehart.

Piaget, J., and Inhelder, B. (1969). *The Psychology of the Child*. Routledge.

Popham, W. J., et al. (1969). *Instructional Objectives* (American Educational Research Association Monograph on Curriculum Evaluation no. 3). Chicago: Rand McNally.

Price, D. J. de Solla (1963). *Little Science, Big Science*. New York: Columbia University Press (new edition 1965).

Provus, M. (1969). 'Evaluation of ongoing programs in the public school system', pp. 242–83 in *Educational Evaluation: New Roles, New Means*, ed. R. W. Tyler (68th Yearbook of the National Society for the Study of Education), part 2. University of Chicago Press.

Reid, J. F. (1975). *Breakthrough in Action: an Independent Evaluation of 'Breakthrough to Literacy'*. Longman.

Rennie, J., Lunzer, E. A., and Williams, W. T. (1974). *Social Education: an Experiment in Four Secondary Schools* (Schools Council Working Paper 51). Evans/Methuen Educational.

Richardson, S. A., Dohrenwend, B., and Klein, D. (1965). *Interviewing: its Forms and Functions*. New York: Basic Books.

Rosenthal, R. (1966). *Experimenter Effects in Behavioral Research*. New York: Appleton-Century.

Schon, D. A. (1971). *Beyond the Stable State: Public and Private Learning in a Changing Society*. Temple Smith.

Schools Council (1965). *Science for the Young School Leaver* (Working Paper 1). Schools Council.

Schools Council/Nuffield Foundation (1970). *The Humanities Project: an Introduction*. Heinemann Educational Books.

Scriven, M. (1967). 'The methodology of evaluation', pp. 39–83 in *Perspectives of Curriculum Evaluation*, by R. W. Tyler, R. M. Gagné and M. Scriven (American Educational Research Association Monograph on Curriculum Evaluation no. 1). Chicago: Rand McNally.

—— (1972). 'Prose and cons about goal-free evaluation', *Evaluation Comment*, **3** (4), 1–4.

Sellitz, C., et al. (1965). *Research Methods in Social Relations*. Methuen.

Sharp, D., et al. (1973). *Attitudes to Welsh and English in the Schools of Wales* (Schools Council Research Studies). Macmillan Education.

Shaw, M. E., and Wright, J. M. (1967). *Scales for Measurement of Attitudes*. McGraw-Hill.

Shipman, M. D. (1972). 'Contrasting views of a curriculum project', *Journal of Curriculum Studies*, **4** (2), 145–53.

Simon, A., and Boyer, E. G., eds (1967–72). *Mirrors for Behavior: an Anthology of Classroom Observation Instruments*, vols 1–6. Philadelphia, Pa: Research for Better Schools.

Smith, E. R., and Tyler, R. W. (1942). *Adventure in American Education*, vol. 3: *Appraising and Recording Student Progress*. New York: Harper.

Smith, L. M. (1971). 'Participant observation and evaluation strategies'. Paper presented to the American Educational Research Association Symposium on Participant Observation and Curriculum: Research and Evaluation, New York, February.

Smith, L. M., and Keith, P. M. (1971). *Anatomy of Educational Innovation*. New York: Wiley.

Smith, L. M., and Pohland, P. A. (1974). 'Education, technology and the rural highlands', pp. 5–54 in *Four Evaluation Examples: Anthropological, Economic, Narrative, and Portrayal*, by R. H. P. Kraft et al. (American Educational Research Association Monograph on Curriculum Evaluation no. 7). Chicago: Rand McNally.

Snyder, B. R. (1971). *The Hidden Curriculum*. New York: Knopf.

Southgate, V., and Lewis, C. Y. (1973). 'How important is the infant reading scheme?' *Reading*, **7** (2), 4–13.

Sparrow, F. H. (1973). 'The role of the evaluator', pp. 1–3 in *Evaluation in Curriculum Development: Twelve Case Studies* (Schools Council Research Studies). Macmillan Education.

Stake, R. E. (1967a). 'The countenance of educational evaluation', *Teachers College Record*, **68** (April), 523–540.

—— (1967b). 'Toward a technology for the evaluation of educational programs', pp. 1–12 in *Perspectives of Curriculum Evaluation*, by R. W. Tyler, R. M. Gagné and M. Scriven (American Educational Research Association Monograph on Curriculum Evaluation no. 1). Chicago: Rand McNally.

—— (1970). 'The decision: does classroom observation belong in an evaluation plan?' pp. 1–5 in *Classroom Observation*, by J. J. Gallagher, G. A. Nuthall and B. Rosenshine (American Educational Research Association Monograph on Curriculum Evaluation no. 6). Chicago: Rand McNally.

—— (1972). 'Responsive evaluation'. Working paper for the Conference on New Approaches to Evaluation, Churchill College, Cambridge (UK), 16–20 December. (Archive copies are held at the Centre for Applied Research in Education, University of East Anglia.)

—— (1973). 'Measuring what learners learn (with a special look at performance contracting)', pp. 193–223 in *School Evaluation*, ed. E. House. Berkeley, Calif.: McCutchan.

—— (1974). 'Responsive evaluation', *New Trends in Evaluation*, **35** (January), 41–73 (Institute of Education, University of Goteborg).

—— (1976). *The Measuring of Education*. Berkeley, Calif.: McCutchan.

Stones, E. (1970). 'Evaluation and the colleges', pp. 13–29 in *Towards Evaluation: Some Thoughts on Tests and Teacher Education*, by E. Stones et al. University of Birmingham School of Education (*Educational Review* Occasional Publication no. 4).

Stufflebeam, D. L. (1969). 'Evaluation as enlightenment for decision-making', pp. 41–73 in *Improving Educational Assessment and an Inventory of Affective Behavior*, ed. W. H. Beatty. Washington, DC: National Education Association.

Stufflebeam, D. L., and Guba, E. (1968). 'Evaluation: the process of stimulating, aiding and abetting insightful action'. Address to the Second National Symposium for Professors of Educational Research, 21 November at Boulder, Colorado. Evaluation Center, College of Education, Ohio State University.

Stufflebeam, D. L., et al. (Phi Delta Kappa National Study Committee on Evaluation) (1971). *Educational Evaluation and Decision Making.* Itasca, Ill.: Peacock.

Suchman, E. A. (1967). *Evaluative Research.* New York: Russell Sage Foundation.

Taba, H. (1962). *Curriculum Development: Theory and Practice.* New York: Harcourt, Brace.

Tawney, D. A. (1973). 'Project Technology', pp. 159–76 in *Evaluation in Curriculum Development: Twelve Case Studies* (Schools Council Research Studies). Macmillan Education.

Tawney, D. A., Swinswood, J. K., and Gunn, S. E. (1973). 'A report to the Schools Council on the formative evaluation of Project Technology'. Presented to the Programme Committee of the Schools Council on 26 June (unpublished).

Tawney, D. A., et al. (1973). 'Evaluators' report on Control Technology'. Report to the Schools Council in January by the Project Technology evaluation unit, based at the University of Keele Department of Education from 1969 to 1972 (unpublished).

Taylor, L. C. (1971). *Resources for Learning.* Harmondsworth: Penguin.

Thorndike, R. L., and Hagen, E. P. (1969). *Measurement and Evaluation in Psychology and Education.* 3rd ed. New York: Wiley.

Travers, R. M. W. (1969). *An Introduction to Educational Research.* 3rd ed. New York: Macmillan. Chapter 8.

Trow, M. A. (1970). 'Methodological problems in the evaluation of innovation', pp. 289–305 in *Problems in the Evaluation of Instruction,* ed. M. C. Wittrock and D. E. Wiley. New York: Holt, Rinehart.

Tukey, J. W. (1963). 'The future of data analysis', *Annals of Mathematical Statistics,* **33,** 13–14.

Tyler, R. W. (1949). *Basic Principles of Curriculum and Instruction.* University of Chicago Press (2nd British impression 1973).

Vernon, P. E. (1956). *The Measurement of Abilities.* 2nd ed. University of London Press.

Walch, W. W., and Walberg, H. J. (1970). 'Pretest and sensitization effects in curriculum evaluation', *American Research Journal,* **7** (4), 605.

Warburton, F. W., and Southgate, V. (1969). *i.t.a.: an Independent Evaluation.* Murray/Chambers.

Warr, P. B., and Knapper, C. (1968). *The Perception of People and Events.* Chichester: Wiley.

Wastnedge, E. R. (1968). 'Whatever happened to Nuffield Junior Science?' *Where,* July supplement. Reprinted on pp. 35–40 in *Problems of Curriculum Innovation,* I, by E. Hoyle and R. Bell. Open University Press, 1972.

Webb, E. J., et al. (1966). *Unobtrusive Measures: Non-Reactive Research in the Social Sciences.* Chicago: Rand McNally.

Westbury, I. (1970). 'Curriculum evaluation', *Review of Educational Research,* **40,** 239–60.

Wiseman, S., and Pidgeon, D. (1970). *Curriculum Evaluation*. Slough: National Foundation for Educational Research.

Wittrock, M. C. (1970). 'The evaluation of instruction: cause-and-effect relations in naturalistic data', pp. 3–21 in *Problems in the Evaluation of Instruction*, ed. M. C. Wittrock and D. E. Wiley. New York: Holt, Rinehart.

Young, M. F. D., ed. (1971). *Knowledge and Control*. Collier-Macmillan (reprinted 1972).

Details of British curriculum projects mentioned in the text

ATTITUDES TO AND MOTIVATION FOR THE LEARNING OF WELSH AND ENGLISH IN WALES

Sponsor: Schools Council (£34 000)
Director: D. W. H. Sharp
Location: Department of Education, University College, Swansea
Duration: 1967–71
Age range: 10+, 12+, 14+
Publisher: Macmillan Education (in Schools Council Research Studies)

BILINGUAL EDUCATION PROJECT

Sponsor: Schools Council (£107 754)
Director: G. E. Richards
Evaluator: C. J. Dodson
Location: Glamorgan Education Committee
Duration: 1968–75
Age range: 5–7+ (pilot study); 5–11 (main project)
Distributor: Welsh Books Council

CAREERS EDUCATION AND GUIDANCE PROJECT

Sponsors: Schools Council (£249 120); industrial and other organizations (£25 800)
Directors: G. Reece, J. Storey (from 1975)
Evaluator: M. Cannon
Location: The Village College, Impington, Cambridge
Duration: 1971–7
Age range: 13–18
Publisher: not yet appointed

COMMUNICATION SKILLS IN EARLY CHILDHOOD

Sponsors: Schools Council (£85 943); N. Ireland Ministry of Education (£2860)
Director: Y. J. Tough
Location: Institute of Education, University of Leeds
Duration: 1973–6
Age range: 3–6
Publisher: Ward Lock Educational/Drake Educational Associates

CONTINUING MATHEMATICS PROJECT

Sponsors: Schools Council (£75 000); Council for Educational Technology (UK) (£35 000); industry (£38 000); Department of Education and Science (£25 000); Scottish Education Department (£2400)
Director: R. W. Morris (from February 1974)
Evaluator: J. Hayter
Location: Mantell Building, University of Sussex
Duration: 1971–6
Age range: 16–18
Publisher: Longman

THE EFFECTIVE USE OF READING

Sponsor: Schools Council (£33 000)
Directors: E. A. Lunzer and W. K. Gardner
Location: School of Education, University of Nottingham
Duration: 1973–6
Age range: 10–14
Publisher: not yet appointed

ENVIRONMENTAL STUDIES PROJECT (5–13)

Sponsor: Schools Council (£67 113)
Director: M. Harris
Evaluator: R. W. Crossland
Location: Cartrefle College of Education, Wrexham, Denbighshire
Duration: 1967–71
Age range: 5–13
Publisher: Rupert Hart-Davis Educational (Granada Publishing)

EXTENDING BEGINNING READING

Sponsor: Schools Council (£36 300)
Director: V. Southgate (Booth)
Location: School of Education, University of Manchester
Duration: 1973–6
Age range: 7–9
Publisher: not yet appointed

GEOGRAPHY 14–18

Sponsors: Schools Council (£79 750); N. Ireland Ministry of Education (£2440)
Director: H. Tolley (from September 1974)
Location: School of Education, University of Bristol
Duration: 1970–5
Age range: 14–18
Publisher: Macmillan Education

HEALTH EDUCATION 5–13

Sponsors: Schools Council (£36 500); Health Education Council (£15 000); Transport and Road Research Laboratory (£31 100)
Director: T. Williams
Location: St Osyth's College of Education, Clacton-on-Sea, Essex
Duration: 1973–6
Age range: 3–15
Publisher: Nelson

HISTORY, GEOGRAPHY AND SOCIAL SCIENCE 8–13

Sponsor: Schools Council (£161 000)
Director: Professor W. A. L. Blyth
Evaluator: K. R. Cooper
Location: School of Education, University of Liverpool
Duration: 1971–5
Age range: 8–13
Publishers: Collins/ESL

HISTORY 13–16

Sponsor: Schools Council (£141 300)
Directors: D. W. Sylvester (to July 1975), A. J. Boddington (from August 1975)
Location: University of Leeds
Duration: 1972–6
Age range: 13–16
Publisher: Holmes McDougall

HUMANITIES CURRICULUM PROJECT

Sponsors: Schools Council (£174 328); Nuffield Foundation (£60 000)
Director: L. A. Stenhouse
Evaluator: B. MacDonald
Location: Centre for Applied Research in Education, University of East Anglia
Duration: 1967–72
Age range: 14–16+
Publisher: Heinemann Educational Books

INITIAL LITERACY PROJECT——see Programme in Linguistics

INTEGRATED SCIENCE PROJECT (SCISP)

Sponsors: School Council (£110 100); N. Ireland Ministry of Education (£4500 for trials in N. Ireland); Associated Examining Board (£12 000 for assessment)
Co-ordinator: M. Lyth (from 1975)
Location: Centre for Science Education, Chelsea College of Science and Technology
Duration: 1969–75
Age range: 13–16
Publisher: Longman

INTEGRATED STUDIES PROJECT

Sponsor: Schools Council (£53 425)
Director: D. Bolam
Evaluator: D. Jenkins
Location: Institute of Education, University of Keele
Duration: 1968–72
Age range: 11–15
Publisher: Oxford University Press

INTER-UNIVERSITY BIOLOGY TEACHING PROJECT

Sponsor: Nuffield Foundation
Co-ordinator: W. H. Dowdeswell
Locations: Universities of Sussex, Bath, Birmingham, Glasgow; Queen Elizabeth College, London, and Chelsea College of Science and Technology, London
Duration: 1969–72
Age range: 18–22
Publishers: Cambridge University Press (Sussex materials)/Longman (Glasgow materials)

I.T.A.: AN INDEPENDENT EVALUATION

Sponsor: Schools Council (£3600)
Directors: Professor F. W. Warburton, V. Southgate (Booth)
Location: Department of Education, University of Manchester
Duration: 1965–8
Age range: 5–8
Publishers: John Murray/W. and R. Chambers

LANGUAGE IN USE—see Programme in Linguistics

MATHEMATICS FOR THE MAJORITY PROJECT

Sponsor: Schools Council (£83 000)
Director: P. Floyd
Evaluators: P. Kaner (1967–71); M. Cannon (1971–2)
Location: Institute of Education, University of Exeter
Duration: 1967–72
Age range: 13–16
Publisher: Chatto & Windus Educational (Granada Publishing)

MATHEMATICS FOR THE MAJORITY CONTINUATION PROJECT

Sponsor: Schools Council (£119 750)
Directors: P. Kaner (1971–4); N. Pass (1975)
Evaluators: G. Manfield (to September 1973), P. Neville (1973), M. Knight (from September 1973)
Location: 3 The Cloisters, Cathedral Close, Exeter
Duration: 1971–5
Age range: 13–16
Publisher: Schofield & Sims

MODERN LANGUAGES PROJECT

Sponsors: Nuffield Foundation (1963–7, under the title Nuffield Foreign Languages Teaching Materials Project); Schools Council (1967–75, £892 000)
Director: D. Rix (from January 1973)
Location: University of York
Age range: 8–16 (French); 11–16 (German, Russian, Spanish)
Publishers: Nuffield introductory materials—E. J. Arnold and Macmillan Education; Schools Council continuation materials—E. J. Arnold

NORTH WEST REGIONAL CURRICULUM DEVELOPMENT PROJECT

Sponsors: Schools Council (until 1970, £30 000); local education authorities (up to £19 000 annually)
Director: W. G. A. Rudd
Location: School of Education, University of Manchester
Duration: 1967–72
Age range: 13–16+
Publishers: Blackie, Holmes McDougall, Macmillan Education, National Foundation for Educational Research; some materials are being distributed from Blackburn Teachers' Centre, Oldham Education Offices and the Curriculum Development Centre at Urmston, Lancashire.

NUFFIELD ADVANCED BIOLOGICAL SCIENCE

Sponsor: Nuffield Foundation
Organizers: P. J. Kelly and W. H. Dowdeswell
Location: (from 1967) Centre for Science Education, Chelsea College of Science
and Technology
Duration: 1965–70
Age range: 16–18
Publisher: Penguin

NUFFIELD JUNIOR SCIENCE

Sponsor: Nuffield Foundation
Organizer: E. R. Wastnedge
Location: Nuffield Foundation, London
Duration: 1964–7
Age range: 5–13
Publisher: Collins

NUFFIELD (O LEVEL) BIOLOGY

Sponsor: Nuffield Foundation (part of the Nuffield Science Teaching Pro-
gramme)
Organizer: W. H. Dowdeswell
Location: Nuffield Foundation, London
Duration: 1962–7
Age range: 11–16
Publishers: Longmans/Penguin

NUFFIELD (O LEVEL) PHYSICS

Sponsor: Nuffield Foundation (part of the Nuffield Science Teaching Pro-
gramme)
Organizer: Professor E. M. Rogers
Location: Nuffield Foundation, London
Duration: 1962–8
Age range: 11–16
Publishers: Longmans/Penguin

NUFFIELD RESOURCES FOR LEARNING PROJECT

Sponsor: Nuffield Foundation
Director: L. C. Taylor
Location: Nuffield Foundation, London
Duration: 1966–71
Age range: 5–18
Publisher: Penguin Education

NUFFIELD SECONDARY SCIENCE

Sponsors: Nuffield Foundation; Schools Council (for evaluation and CSE Mode III work, £9000)
Organizer: H. Misselbrook
Evaluator: D. J. Alexander
Location: (from 1967) Centre for Science Education, Chelsea College of Science and Technology
Duration: 1965–70 (evaluation 1969–70)
Age range: 13–16
Publisher: Longman

OXFORD PRIMARY SCIENCE RESEARCH PROJECT (AN ENQUIRY INTO THE FORMATION OF SCIENTIFIC CONCEPTS IN CHILDREN 5–13)

Sponsors: Department of Education and Science (£16 000 approx.); Research Unit, Institute of Education, University of Bristol (for evaluation)
Leader: S. Redman
Evaluator: W. Harlen
Location: Institute of Education, University of Oxford
Duration: 1963–7 (evaluation 1966–7)
Age range: 5–13
Publisher: Institute of Education, University of Oxford (main report); Institute of Education, University of Bristol (evaluation report)

PROGRAMME IN LINGUISTICS AND ENGLISH TEACHING: INITIAL LITERACY PROJECT

Sponsors: Nuffield Foundation (1964–7); Schools Council (1967–70, £152 500 shared between sections of the programme); Centre for Research in Educational Sciences, University of Edinburgh (for evaluation)
Director: Professor M. A. K. Halliday (until December 1970)
Organizer, Initial Literacy Project: D. Mackay
Evaluator: J. F. Reid
Location: Department of General Linguistics, University College, London
Duration: 1964–70 (evaluation 1969–70)
Age range: 5–7
Publisher: Longman

PROGRAMME IN LINGUISTICS AND ENGLISH TEACHING: LANGUAGE IN USE PROJECT

Sponsors: Nuffield Foundation (1964–7); Schools Council (1967–71, £152 500 shared between sections of the programme)
Directors: Professor M. A. K. Halliday (until December 1970); P. Doughty (from January 1971)
Evaluator: J. Pearce
Location: Department of General Linguistics, University College, London
Duration: 1964–71
Age range: 11–18+
Publisher: Edward Arnold

PROGRESS IN LEARNING SCIENCE

Sponsor: Schools Council (£51 000)
Director: W. Harlen
Location: School of Education, University of Reading
Duration: 1973–7
Age range: 5–13
Publisher: not yet appointed

PROJECT PHI

Sponsor: Scottish Education Department (£22 371)
Director: M. Roebuck
Location: Department of Education, University of Glasgow
Duration: 1970–4
Age range: 11–18
Materials used: from the Scottish Integrated Science scheme

PROJECT TECHNOLOGY

Sponsor: Schools Council (£270 000 + £17 263 for evaluation)
Director: G. B. Harrison
Evaluator: D. A. Tawney
Location: Loughborough College of Education
Duration: 1967–72
Age range: 11–18
Publishers: Heinemann Educational Books and English Universities Press; project-initated journals from the National Centre for School Technology, Trent Polytechnic, Nottingham

SAFARI (SUCCESS AND FAILURE AND RECENT INNOVATION)

Sponsor: Ford Foundation (£46 000)
Director: B. MacDonald
Location: Centre for Applied Research in Education, University of East Anglia
Duration: 1973–6
Age range: 13–16
Publisher: Open Books

SCIENCE 5–13

Sponsors: Schools Council (£146 700); Nuffield Foundation (£18 000); Scottish Education Department (£10 340); Plastics Institute (£2000)
Director: L. F. Ennever
Evaluator: W. Harlen
Location: School of Education, University of Bristol
Duration: 1967–75
Age range: 5–13
Publisher: Macdonald Educational

SIXTH FORM MATHEMATICS CURRICULUM PROJECT

Sponsor: Schools Council (£113 185)
Director: C. P. Ormell
Location: School of Education, University of Reading
Duration: 1969–76
Age range: 16–18
Publisher: Heinemann Educational Books

UNCAL (UNDERSTANDING COMPUTER ASSISTED LEARNING)

Sponsor: Department of Education and Science (£94 000)
Director: Barry MacDonald
Location: Centre for Applied Research in Education, University of East Anglia
Duration: 1973–6
Focus: the National Development Programme in Computer Assisted Learning

Notes on contributors

KEITH COOPER read history at Oxford, and taught in comprehensive schools in Kirby and central Liverpool. From 1971 to 1975 he was the evaluator of the Schools Council project on History, Geography and Social Science 8–13; from 1973 to 1975 he acted as Chairman of the Schools Council evaluators' group. He is now at the North Riding College of Education, Scarborough. His first research was into the problem of the school as an organization; his current concerns are with the diffusion of curriculum ideas, and with the use of philosophy in curriculum development and evaluation.

MICHAEL ERAUT took his Ph.D. in chemistry at Cambridge in 1965, before switching to education, with special reference to curriculum and teaching problems in higher education. For two years he was Assistant Professor at the University of Illinois. In 1967 he joined the University of Sussex and initiated the present M.A. course in cirriculum development and educational technology. He is particularly concerned with in-service education and curriculum decision-making in schools; his research has included evaluation studies within the university, the devising of techniques for the analysis of curriculum materials, and participation in curriculum projects (as a developer rather than an evaluator). He is now Director of the university's Centre for Educational Technology.

DAVID HAMILTON taught for three years in a Leicestershire comprehensive school after graduating in geology at Edinburgh University. In 1969 he returned to Edinburgh as a research student in the Centre for Research in the Educational Sciences, where he developed a prior interest in the school-based consequences of curriculum innovation, in a Ph.D. thesis (1973). During 1972–4 he worked as a temporary lecturer in the Department of Education, University of Glasgow, investigating (with others) the use of self-instructional science materials in small secondary schools in the highlands and islands of Scotland (Project PHI). He has attempted throughout to develop theoretical perspectives and methodological procedures adequate to the phenomena being studied. His current interests include classroom research, curriculum evaluation, multivariate statistics and the history of educational research.

WYNNE HARLEN graduated in physics at Oxford and taught science in schools and as a science lecturer at St Mary's College, Cheltenham. Between 1962 and

1965 she studied part-time for an M.A. in education, carrying out research into the development of children's scientific concepts. In 1966–7 she conducted an evaluation of the Oxford Primary Science Research Project, going on to become evaluator of the Science 5–13 Project from its beginning in 1967 until 1973, since when she has been director of the Progress in Learning Science Project. During her time with Science 5–13, she completed a Ph.D. dissertation on formative curriculum evaluation. She is the author of *Science 5–13: a Formative Evaluation* and has contributed to *Evaluation in Curriculum Development: Twelve Case Studies*—both in the Schools Council Research Studies series.

BARRY MACDONALD has since 1970 been Senior Lecturer in Educational Evaluation in the University of East Anglia's Centre for Applied Research in Education. He is currently directing two investigative programmes: SAFARI, a study of the medium-term effects of curriculum innovation, and UNCAL, an evaluation study of the National Development Programme in Computer Assisted Learning. A former primary school teacher and college lecturer in educational theory, he entered the field of evaluation in 1968, when he was appointed evaluator of the Schools Council/Nuffield Foundation Humanities Curriculum Project. He has since published a number of articles and co-edited several books concerned with evaluation and research; he was a contributor to *Evaluation in Curriculum Development: Twelve Case Studies*.

MALCOLM PARLETT undertook postgraduate research in experimental psychology at King's College, Cambridge, followed by two years' postdoctoral research in educational psychiatry in the United States. During 1968–73 he served as Lecturer in Educational Sciences at the University of Edinburgh, and in 1973–4 he was Visiting Associate Professor in the Education Division of Massachusetts Institute of Technology. He is now at Wolfson College, Oxford, and works part-time with the National Foundation for Educational Research (running an illuminative evaluation of the education of the visually handicapped) and with the Nuffield Group for Research and Innovation in Higher Education.

STEPHEN STEADMAN graduated in physics at Manchester University and joined the Meteorological Office for a short period before turning to teaching. After six years of teaching experience he was reading for a higher degree when he took a post researching into student wastage at Manchester and Salford Universities. From that post he came as a Research Officer to the Schools Council, where he has worked since late 1972, advising on evaluation procedures.

DAVID TAWNEY graduated in natural sciences at Cambridge in 1953 and gained a Certificate in Education there a year later. After teaching physics in schools in the United Kingdom and abroad for twelve years, he joined the Education Department at the University of Keele as a methods tutor and played a major part in developing the undergraduate course in science education and in establishing the Keele Science and Technology Centre. While at Keele, he directed an independent evaluation study of the Schools Council's Project Technology, was a Topic Leader in the Nuffield-funded Science Teacher Education Project, and became Secretary of the Education Group of the Institute of Physics. In 1974 he joined the Centre for Applied Research in Education at the University of East Anglia to take part in the evaluation of the National Development Programme in Computer Assisted Learning. He contributed two chapters to *Evaluation in Curriculum Development: Twelve Case Studies.*

Index